J. P. Clark

Twayne's World Authors Series
African Literature

Bernth Lindfors, Editor
The University of Texas at Austin

TWAS 734

J. P. CLARK
(1935-   )
Photograph by Sunmi Smart-Cole

J. P. Clark

By Robert M. Wren

University of Houston

Twayne Publishers • *Boston*

J. P. Clark

Robert M. Wren

Copyright © 1984 by G.K. Hall & Company
All Rights Reserved
Published by Twayne Publishers
A Division of G. K. Hall & Company
70 Lincoln Street
Boston, Massachusetts 02111

Printed on permanent/durable acid-free paper and bound in the United States of America.

Library of Congress Cataloging in Publication Data

Wren, Robert M.
J.P. Clark.

(Twayne's world authors series; 734)
Bibliography: p. 171
Includes index.
1. Clark, John Pepper, 1935-   —Criticism and interpretation.
2. Nigeria in literature.
I. Title. II. Title: J.P. Clark.
III. Series: Twayne's world authors series ; TWAS 734.
PR9387.9.C55Z94   1984   828
83-13018
ISBN 0-8057-6581-6

Contents

About the Author

Preface

Chronology

    CHAPTER ONE
    Clark's Nigeria   1

    CHAPTER TWO
    The Ibadan Years   23

    CHAPTER THREE
    Clark's Parvin Year   54

    CHAPTER FOUR
    The Ozidi Complex   87

    CHAPTER FIVE
    Casualties   128

    CHAPTER SIX
    Prospects   158

Notes and References   163

Selected Bibliography   171

Index   176

About the Author

Robert M. Wren, Professor of English at the University of Houston, was Visiting Senior Lecturer at the University of Lagos in Nigeria 1972-1975. The English Department, in which Wren taught Shakespeare, American literature, and African literature, was headed at that time by J. P. Clark, subject of this book. Over these years a cordial relationship developed between Wren and Clark, which continues to the present.

Prior to visiting at Lagos, Wren was a specialist in Shakespeare and the Elizabethan drama. He completed his doctorate at Princeton University and published extensively in the field. He headed the drama department at the State University of New York at Binghamton, and has directed many plays, including Clark's The Masquerade.

Since teaching at Lagos, Wren has written numerous articles on Nigerian literature, and his book Achebe's World, on the cultural and historical context of the novels of Chinua Achebe, has been well received (published in America by Three Continents Press, 1980, and abroad by Longman, 1981).

He is currently engaged in a study of the intellectual milieu of the Ibadan writers of the 1940s through 1960s.

Preface

J. P. Clark, universally acknowledged to be one of Africa's foremost authors, has never before been the subject of a full-length study, or of any study that has taken into account the full range of his literary work. Clark is a poet, playwright, journalist, translator, and essayist. In every form he has been notable, and is a poet and playwright of the first rank in both originality and in expressive power.

Clark's literary career has been largely--indeed overwhelmingly--devoted to the expression of African tradition through the medium of the English language. He devoted years to accumulating, transcribing, adapting, and translating the greatest of the epics of the Niger Delta, Ozidi's heroic tale. All of his work, with rare exceptions, is based on the manners, customs, and imagery of the people and lands of Nigeria.

This book will review Clark's work in rough chronological order. The first chapter, however, is in part an ethnographic review of the Western Niger Delta land and people, and an account of Clark's own origins. Subsequent chapters will deal with his artistic beginnings at the University of Ibadan, including his first volume of poems and first published play; with his year in America and the book, plays, and poems produced that year; with the play, translation, and film he created from the tale of Ozidi; and with his poems on the Nigerian crises and conflict of the 1960s. It includes, finally, a note on his newest work (not yet published at this time).

I am indebted to Clark for his cooperation and for permission to quote from his works. Chinua Achebe gave permission to quote from one of his poems. Michael Echeruo was kind enough to share with me some recollections of student days and also criticized the chapter on Casualties and made valuable suggestions, some of which I was able to act upon. Bernth Lindfors has, as always, been an inspiration and a help. Hilda Jaffe read the manuscript and made many valuable suggestions. Not least among the others whom I should mention here are the staff of the University of Houston Magnetic Implementation Center for their unfailing courtesy and diligence in translating my manuscript into readable type.

Robert M. Wren

<u>University of Houston</u>

Chronology

1935   Johnson Pepper Clark born at Kiagbodo, Warri Province, Western Region (the Province is now in Bendel State), Nigeria, April 6. Son of Chief Clark Fuludu Bekederemo and his wife, Poro, daughter of Amakashe Adomi.

1941   Entered Native Administration School, Okrika (Ofonibengha, on the Forcados River), Burutu Local Government Area; continued until 1948.

1948   Attended Native Administration School, Jeremi (Otu-Ughienvwen), Ughelli Local Government Area. Entered Government College, Ughelli (Cambridge School Leaving Certificate 1954).

1954/1955   Clerk, Office of the Chief Secretary to the Government of Nigeria.

1955   Matriculated, University College, Ibadan (UCI).

1956   Editor, UCI Students' Union journal, the Beacon.

1957   Founding editor, UCI poetry journal, the Horn.

1960   B.A. (honors) in English, UCI. Nigeria becomes independent, October 1.

1960/1961   Information Officer, Ministry of Information, Ibadan.

1961   Poems published, Mbari Publications, Ibadan. Song of a Goat published, Mbari.

1961/1962   Head of Features and Editorial Writer, Express Group of Newspapers, Lagos.

J. P. CLARK

1962/1963	Parvin Fellow, Princeton University, U.S.A.
1963/1964	Research Fellow, Institute of African Studies, University of Ibadan.
1963	Recorded Okabou version of The Ozidi Saga, October; recorded Afoluwa version, November; recorded and filmed Erivini version, December.
1964	Three Plays published, Oxford University Press. Appointed Lecturer, English Department, University of Lagos. America Their America published, Andre Deutsch, London. Married Ebun Odutola. Daughter Ebiere born.
1965	A Reed in the Tide published, Longman, London.
1966	Military coups d'etat in Nigeria, January 15 and July 29. Ozidi (play) published, Oxford. Became coeditor (with Abiola Irele) of Black Orpheus (resigned full editorship 1975/1976).
1967-1970	Civil War in Nigeria.
1968	Round-the-world trip. Daughter Tamara born.
1970	Casualties published, Longman. The Example of Shakespeare (essays) published, Longman.
1971	Daughter Imoyadue born.
1972	Appointed Professor of English, University of Lagos, February.
1975/1976	Visiting Distinguished Fellow, Center for the Humanities, Wesleyan University in Connecticut.
1977	The Ozidi Saga published, Oxford and Ibadan University Press.
1978	Son Ambakederemo born.

Chronology

1980   Retired as Professor of English; resumed residence at Kiagbodo.

1981   A Decade of Tongues (poems) published, Longman. The Boat (play) performed. State of the Union (poems) completed.

1982   Established PEC Repertory Theatre at Lagos.

Chapter One
Clark's Nigeria

Nigeria was certainly inhabited long before the first dated archaeological remains were deposited--about 40,000 years ago. The record is only recently being established. It shows early occupation north of the forest belt; the people were probably hunters and gatherers. The broad forest belt seems not to have been penetrated until comparatively recent times, perhaps four to five thousand years ago. The development of technologies for the growing of yams and the extraction of palm oil from the oil palm tree was necessary before the forest areas could be made suitable for settled human life. The need for still newer technologies for the exploitation of water resources meant that the last area to be occupied was the southernmost forest, the delta region of the great River Niger (1). It may be that the delta people, the Ijo̱ (or Ijaw) of southern Nigeria, are the oldest inhabitants of the entire territory. They are the stock that produced J. P. Clark.

Clark is not, it must be clear from the start, a provincial writer. He is Nigerian more than simply Ijo̱. The north, the west, and the east of Nigeria have all inspired his poems. Yet it would be surprising if his own people were not his greatest inspiration, and indeed they are. They may originally have been pioneers who moved south, opening new technologies in agriculture, or they may have been the victims of latecomers who forced them to make way in lands they settled first. In either case, in recent times they fully adapted to the circumstances of the country. Their adaptation and their environment shaped them of course, and shaped Clark's art in large measure as well.

The Niger Delta

The environment needs to be understood both for its influence on Clark's art and for its role in defining

1

the culture from which he came. The Niger delta is an
immense complex, with thousands of swamps, creeks,
rivers, and estuaries that have been formed in recent
geologic time. The best habitable land lies generally
twenty to thirty miles from the narrow sand bar that
borders the Atlantic. That sand bar is pierced by
estuaries having old and romantic names. The Benin,
Escravos, Forcados, Ramos, Nun, Brass, Sombreiro, New
Calabar, Bonny, and Adoni Rivers were named by Portuguese and other traders who dared not travel far from
the thin bar, fearful of the near-certain death from
mal-aria--bad air, as superstition had it. The area
between the ocean and highland came to be peopled by
fishermen, exploiting the vast food resources of the
mangrove swamps between good land and ocean sands.

Trade made necessary coastal trading ports, like the
towns called Forcados, Brass, and Bonny, yet, except
for the last, the coastal ports tended to remain just
ports, while the controlling population centers clung
to higher ground, less subject to annual floods. The
Ijo were, and are, land folk who take their living
from the rivers and creeks, not the sea.

The lines that separate sand bar from mangrove, and
mangrove from farm land, are fairly clearly demarcated.
Also stable are the estuaries--early maps of the coast
and newer ones do not differ greatly in general outline. But within that stability there have been many
shifts of sand bars, rivers, creeks, and, with the
creeks, islands and swamp areas. Every year the rains
swell the great river to floods that inundate all the
lower lands of the delta and deposit vast amounts of
new effluvium, sometimes extending habitable land and
sometimes removing it. All marginal areas are subject
to annual change. In rare years of great floods significant changes occur, and occasionally the people themselves reorganize the flow of the rivers. One such
change three hundred years ago altered the economic
life of Clark's ancestral clan. It will be discussed
later.

It might be said generally that the Ijo people
inhabit swampland, land that is river- or creek-side
during dry seasons and at least partly inundated at
flood time. The major differences lie between fresh-
water and salt-water swamp. The latter is agricultural-
ly poor mangrove territory. Some of the fresh-water
swampland is actually mainland. In either case, the

central economic factors in all Ijo communities are
the water and the canoe that floats upon it.

The economy of the delta depends primarily upon
resources from the water. Agriculture is limited by
the fact that comparatively little Ijo territory is
suitable for growth of the forest belt staple crop, the
yam. In fresh-water areas, plantain and oil palm grow
plentifully and cassava cultivation is extensive, but
the great ecological advantage of the entire region is
the supply of fish and shellfish. The mangrove belt,
though despised by colonials for its monotony, its
insects, and its odor, is immensely rich in protein
resources. As a result the Ijo people are uncommonly
strong and handsome. They are also suppliers of fish
to the peoples of the yam belt, with whom they trade.

The location of the Ijo people made them natural
middlemen when trade from the Atlantic began to supplement traditional commerce to the north. Indeed, migration of Ijo to the Western Delta seems to have been
coincidental in time with the first visits in the
fifteenth century by Portuguese merchants to the delta
coast. There is no necessary connection between the
arrival of the Europeans and African migrations. There
is general evidence of migrations throughout nearby
West Africa. The causes are varied and only partly
understood; population pressure was significant but its
extent is unclear. Whatever the causes, traditions
still reported in the delta tell of quarrels which led
to the displacement of groups and the establishment of
new settlements at some distance from the places of
origin. Such migrations seem to have meant that, by
around the beginning of the sixteenth century, all of
the mainland bordering the mangrove belt was settled by
the ancestors of the people living in the areas today.

The response of the delta people to the European
contact varied. At Bonny, on the sand bar itself, east
of the southernmost point of the delta, a powerful
city-state arose. Farther west, the Nembe kingdom
established another powerful trading state, but at some
distance from the sea. Yet farther west are found the
Central Delta Ijo, who seem to be the primary stock
from which the other Ijo branched. Their trade,
appropriately enough, was largely among other Ijo
communities and with neighbors to the north. Clark's
Western Delta Ijo traded with the Europeans through
their outpost, Forcados, at the edge of the area. As a

result, their association with Europe has been greatly
overshadowed by neighboring Warri, the Itsekiri trading
city, inland on the west branch of the Forcados River.
   Nevertheless, Clark's home, Kiagbodo, had a significant role in the trade, and members of Clark's family
are remembered as highly influential personages in the
Western Delta.

Kiagbodo History

   Kiagbodo lies in the extreme north of the Western
Delta, near the confluence of the Kiagbodo River and
the east branch of the great Niger tributary, the
Forcados. Kiagbodo's position resembles a peninsula
piercing the mainland territories of the Itsekiri,
Urhobo, and Isoko peoples. Indeed, relations with the
Urhobo are so close that most Kiagbodo men are bilingual in Urhobo and Ijo. Commonly wives who are
married from outside are Urhobo women, as was the case
with Clark's grandmother--to whom one of his most
admired poems is addressed.
   Kiagbodo is the capital of the Ngbilebiri branch of
the Mein ibe, or "clan" as it is generally called in
English. The history of Ngbilebiri provides some
insight into the migrations of five hundred years ago,
as well as into Clark's own sense of the past. The
history begins with Mein, ancestor of the very large
and dispersed clan. He and his wife, Obolu, are said
to have lived at Benin. Benin, in the mid-fifteenth
century, was troubled by civil war, and civil war was
followed by military activities that scattered the war
leaders and their troops, significantly depopulating
the famous imperial city (2). Tradition describes
Mein's departure from Benin as resulting from internal
Benin conflict. He settled at Aboh, a trade center
located near the delta's northern peak. According to
some Ngbilebiri tradition, Ngbile was Mein's son, but
other apparently older traditions assert that Mein had
many children at Aboh, one of whom was named Kor (or
Koo). Mein killed a woman at Aboh because she
violated his god Dirimegbeya; he fled with his family
to Ogobiri, on a tributary of the Nun River. This move
placed Mein at the edge between Central and Western
Ijo.
   Kor succeeded his father as family head. One of his
sons, Ogo, remained at Ogobiri. Other sons, however,

migrated west: Kalanama founded Akugbene Mein; Ngbile founded Kiagbodo; Ogbulu founded the town and subclan named after him. All three towns are located on the Forcados River, Kiagbodo being northernmost and Akugbene downstream, with Ogbodobiri between. Together these three subclans of Mein controlled the fresh-water creeks of the Forcados system while their cousins at Ogobiri remained the eldest branch of the family and lived away to the east.

The Mein migration and spread is not unique in its pattern among the Ijo moving out from the Central Delta region, but the connection with Benin renders it in several ways among the most interesting migrations. Some people imagine that "Africa has no history, except colonization," as it has been put by supercilious colonials. The Mein migration disproves the contention, and the story of Benin and its relation to such peoples as Ngbilebiri Mein deserves further study. In general, what is relevant to Clark's world can be told rather simply:

Benin was beyond any doubt a great city. When Portuguese visited it in 1485 the city itself had been reduced by the internal conflicts mentioned earlier. Nevertheless the empire extended from Cotonu in the West (for this reason the nation of which Cotonu is the capital is called Benin today) to the Bonny River in the East (but not enclosing the Ijo regions, the delta east of the Forcados), and at one time or another its influence extended to Onitsha, west across the Niger. During the centuries that followed the Portuguese visit, until the British sack of Benin in 1897, the city flourished. Even today, when hero tales (like Clark's *Ozidi*) are told, they are set in Benin. As Clark has put it, "Ado, the other name for Benin City, . . . to the Ijo imagination, is the embodiment of all that is distant and mysterious, the empire of improbable happenings that together with the world of spirits help to explain the events of their own lives" (3). The mysterious city also had real temporal and spiritual power in the minds of Clark's ancestors, as their deference to it attests.

Not only does tradition assign a Benin origin to Mein, but Mein's grandsons who founded Kiagbodo and Akugbene are said to have returned to Benin to secure for themselves authority over their lands on the Forcados. This was granted, and today at the two towns the symbols of Benin authority are still held. These include remarkable bronze or brass objects, notably two small (about five inches high) representations of the human face (4).

The importance of Kiagbodo Mein throughout the Forcados River creeks cannot have been based on Benin authority, however, because (except for some settlements west of the Forcados) the Ijo̱ were not subject to Benin or even threatened with subjugation so far as is known. Yet Ijo̱ in other parts of the delta called the Forcados "Mei̱n to̱ru̱" or river of the Mein. Traditionally the Ngbilebiri Mein of Kiagbodo claim the Forcados River trade as their own, from the Nun River conjunction to the sea. Kiagbodo's success in establishing itself in control of the slave trade seems well enough established historically to warrant an explanation.

E. J. Alagoa, the historian who has studied the traditions of the delta peoples most extensively, calls attention to the fact that originally the Kabowei controlled the slave trade on the Forcados, having a station on the estuary near their home, farther upstream than the Mein. A rumor that European ships would attack upstream during flood season caused the Kabowei, with help from neighbors, to dam the river and divert its course. The result, unforeseen at the time, was to relinquish the profitable trade to Mein control. Later the Kabowei (after a war with the Mein) improved their position by establishing themselves at a new town, Patani, which remains their capital (5).

Neither the Kabowei nor the Mein occupied the coastal area where the trade took place, though it must be assumed that their fresh-water home territories gave them the resources to deal effectively with the coastal Ijo̱. In the later nineteenth century the British Niger Company accepted the Ngbilebiri Mein (Kiagbodo) claim to control of the Forcados to the sea.

A final note to this historical account is needed to show the relation of Clark's origins to the tale of Ozidi, which has played such a large role in Clark's artistic career. Ozidi's origin is said to have been a trance vision of the high priest of the great god of the Tarakiri i̱be at Orua (Saga, xx). The Tarakiri are like the Mei̱n in several respects. Their ancestor, Tara, was the son of Ondo. Ondo lived at Benin but, like Mein, went to live at Aboh. Thence he migrated to the same creek where Mein settled at Ogobiri. War with the Mein led to a migration that was unsuccessful in establishing a permanent home; a second move brought them to Orua (6). There, they are today still neighbors of Ogobiri Mein, but well to the southeast of Kiagbodo. The waterside community is the subject of Clark's Ozidi film, Tides of the Delta (discussed below in Chapter 4).

Kiagbodo Life

The account of the manner of life in Clark's homeland that follows is drawn largely from Philip E. Leis, who has written the most useful anthropological study available in English (7). It deals with growing up in a remote, isolated village, well to the east of Kiagbodo. Leis's material has been adapted to describe somewhat better circumstances in the less remote Kiagbodo environment. Additional material is drawn from an unpublished commentary on Clark's dramas by Francis R. Ugo (1979) and from the present writer's own research.

A central circumstance cannot be emphasized too strongly: Ijo life is near or in the water virtually from birth. Children learn to swim almost as soon as they learn to walk. Access to the water is, as often as not, via canoe. The canoe is not only used for transport; it serves as a pier, its edge is a convenient toilet seat, it is a refuge in flood, and it facilitates in various ways the major industry— fishing. In former times great war canoes dominated the rivers, in commerce or in battle. In recent years they have been used only for ceremony and festivals. Above all, the canoe is the means for almost all productive and social activity beyond the village itself. When the river is in flood and the creeks are full, intercommunity life is at full as well. When the dry season drains the creeks, then only the river remains, and those who lack easy access are comparatively isolated.

Clark recalls childhood voyages among the creeks with his mother's mother, the canoe loaded with "tapioca"—cassava products (and other produce)—and propelled by a hired servant. "Granny" was Urhobo, of mainland stock, and she traded for fish. Her voyages to distant markets might last five to nine days, threading slowly among the intricate creeks, while the child assisted by bailing water when necessary (8). No doubt the experience helped to ingrain the imagery that would dominate his poetry.

That his maternal grandmother should be Urhobo is not surprising. Kiagbodo men have been marrying their neighboring women for many generations. Such marriages are of great significance in the ordering of domestic society, and a fuller explanation is essential background to domestic aspects of Clark's plays.

The great societal organization at Kiagbodo is, as was seen above, the <u>ibe</u> (or clan), which is Mein, subclan, Ngbilebiri. Kiagbodo itself is composed of several subsections called <u>ama</u>, or villages. Within the <u>ama</u>, the various <u>wari</u>, or families, have their heads and are "extended"; that is, the family elder or head leads a group which includes collateral relatives as well as descendants. Each male is expected at some time to marry, as is each female. The nature and conditions of marriage depend upon the kind of marriage that is contracted.

Most marriages are local. That is, a man and a woman from different lineages within the clan are married. The wife in such a marriage is <u>kie-ere</u>. This signifies that she and her husband meet as equals (more or less), and her children are in fact her own. They do not belong to her husband, and their closest familial connections are with their maternal relatives. Thus it is that young Clark was so close to his mother's mother--a circumstance duplicated in the hero saga of <u>Ozidi</u>. As Leis puts it, the local wife is connected by only a "small dowry." To her husband she is <u>kala ikiya</u>, or "small friend."

In contrast, a wife cannot be gotten so cheaply from outside the clan. (A local wife who required a large dowry, or bride price, would lose her independence; hence the common refusal of local women to allow any large dowry to be paid for them.) Leis calls the "big dowry" wife <u>fe ere</u>, or purchased woman, and describes her role as virtually that of slave. Clark uses the term <u>bra-ere</u>, defining it as "hand maid" (<u>Saga</u>, xxxiv). In either case, both wife and child belong to the husband outright. They are his personal possessions and he can dispose of them as he sees fit. The child of a <u>bra-ere</u> may be sold, or instead he may inherit. The child of a <u>kie-ere</u> has no claim on his father's estate or rank, while the <u>bra-ere</u> son may become, if his father is a king, king himself.

There are, strictly speaking, no "kings" among the
Ijo. In a characteristic community, there are various terms for leadership. An influential person
(whether war leader or champion wrestler) is called
alotu. A specially designated figure is the "owner"
or "mayor" of the town, the amananawei. In Clark's
play Ozidi the amananawei Ewiri is influential but
not powerful. Such a role seems typical of the office.
The ibenanawei is the clan chief, who is closest to
"king" at Kiagbodo. That office is now held by Clark's
own father, Chief Clark Fuludu Bekederemo. A final
office, pere, was held, when Clark was born, by
Duudei. After his death in 1944 the office remained
vacant; only very recently was it filled.

Pere requires a brief explanation because it is
the office of "king" that Temugedege in Ozidi assumes
(to his own misfortune and that of his brother). At
Kiagbodo, the first pere was Ngbile, who is said to
have secured the title through award by the Oba of
Benin. But pere is not a Benin office, and, upon
Ngbile's death, leadership of the clan and the office
of pere were divided. Further, while pere customarily is the High Priest of the great god of the clan,
at Kiagbodo the pere could not be High Priest of
Dirimoagbiya (the Mein god) as there were other pere
at Ogobiri and at the other Mein settlements on the
Forcados. At Orua, of course, the pere was the High
Priest; it was a pere who is said to have been
inspired with the creation of the Ozidi tale. In any
case, the pere holds a spiritual function, and as a
result would wield some political power. His authority
in secular matters would not inherently be great, but
would depend upon the personality of the priest.

The clan god is not, of course, the supreme God.
The distant, supreme maternal deity is, according to
Leis, Wonyinghi. Clark calls her Tamara, "She Who
Creates." In either case She is female. Generally She
is remote, like the High God Chinua Achebe describes in
chapter 21 of Things Fall Apart (1958):

> We make sacrifices to the little gods, but when they
> fail and there is no one else to turn to we go to
> Chukwu. It is right to do so. We approach a great
> man through his servants. But when his servants
> fail to help us, then we go to the last source of
> hope.

Clark's Tamara is no doubt similar, but the great
powers of Oreame, Ozidi's grandmother, give her direct
access to Oyin, "Our Mother," by which name She is
also known (Saga, xxxiv).
  Oreame's great powers are beyond those of the
village diviners, whom Leis calls buroyou. Rather
Oreame resembles the more dangerous--indeed terrible--
diriguoyou. Both are commonly women, but the latter
are usually bra-ere wives, strangers and therefore
dangerous. This suits Oreame well; she has great power
in Orua, but is no native of the place (Saga, 12).
  Another spiritual entity identified by Leis is
teme, which he identifies with "soul," but teme
probably is closer to Igbo chi, the "personal god"
who determines one's role and success in life, and to
the Ewe se. This latter spirit, as described by Kofi
Awoonor, sends the individual into the world with a
mission. Nevertheless, infinite possibilities exist,
through charms, magic, propitiation, and the like to
alter se's mission for the better, or perhaps the
worse (9). The Ijo concept provides an insight clari-
fying both the Igbo and Ewe concepts. Before one's
birth, teme makes an agreement with the supreme
deity. This agreement determines the future life of
the individual. A wise teme, of course, will make a
good agreement; but, unfortunately, before birth the
spirit is too young to bargain well, and may even be
foolish. Thus one may be compelled throughout life to
contend with the mistake of one's own personal god. It
can be a heavy burden.
  Ancestors and other gods have spiritual existence
among the Ijo. Ancestors, or duwoiyou according to
Leis, are an important part of one's life, especially
if they are honored and shown respect through sacrifice. Oru or orumo are local gods. They, like
ancestors, may be embodied in masks. These manifesta-
tions are common throughout southern Nigeria, under
various names. More distinctive to the Ijo people
are owumo. These are water spirits, who require a
good deal of special attention, as in the opening of
Clark's play Ozidi. Owumo are often embodied in
masquerades; the most common representations are
modeled on fish shapes or abstracted from them.
Orumo on the other hand are promised gifts for personal services, such as giving children to barren women.
  The barrenness of Ebiere at the start of Clark's

play Song of a Goat might be treated by an appeal to an orumo--except that she knows the fault lies not in her but in her husband. Nevertheless she is induced to do as barren Ijo women do, to call upon a masseur, or iyololi. The iyololi, or "presser," Leis says, puts the "womb into proper positioning by violent kneading and twisting." Other means to induce conception involve close association with very young children so that their presence may, by sympathetic magic, bring the desired result. Similarly, a frog with skin smooth as a child's might be worn in the barren woman's lappa in the same way a child is carried.

Once born, the child, as was said earlier, belongs either to his father or mother, depending on his mother's status. If, as in Clark's case, the child's mother is kie-ere, the mother may give the weaned infant to its grandmother to care for. So common is this arrangement that nene, mother, is normally reserved for the grandmother, while the child calls his mother by her proper name. This is reflected in the identification of the grandmother in Ozidi as "mother" while the mother is merely "Orea."

Family, whether in maternal or paternal line, is of great importance among the Ijo, as it is among peoples everywhere in the world. Family has, however, special significance among the Ijo, because religious as well as social and political considerations are involved. It was noted earlier that at Kiagbodo, the offices of pere and clan chief are divided. Each, however, is inherited, and at an earlier point Ngibele held both positions (indeed there was apparently no distinction between them). Inheritance of these positions can proceed only through a bra-ere (large dowry) marriage. As one consequence, such marriages are seen to have great significance for the bride as well as the groom. Clark, in The Masquerade, shows the strikingly adverse reaction of a father, about to grant his daughter in a large dowry marriage, to the discovery that the groom's birth was tainted.

Birth can be tainted in a variety of ways. Sexual intercourse under deviant conditions requires propitiation if the families involved are not to be cursed. Ugo in his monograph on Clark's dramas points out that incest (as in Clark's Song of a Goat) requires rites of atonement. "The village elders and . . . selected kinsmen of the sinner sit together in the grove of the ancestors" for the slaughter of perhaps a goat, as well as sacrifice of kola, chalk, palm wine, gin, coconut and cowries, or some combination of these. A similar sacrifice is required after intercourse in a grove dedicated to a god. The sacrifice relieves danger not only to the guilty couple but to their parents, siblings, and children. The sacrifice of a goat in <u>Song of a Goat</u> has terrible consequences because it is performed for the wrong reason. It, in turn, helps to produce the curse that troubles characters in <u>The Masquerade</u>.

Another tainted birth Ugo discusses is that of an uncircumcised mother. Ugo does not make it clear whether practice has changed since former times, but points out that quite recently a family forcibly circumcised a pregnant woman whose religious scruples had prevented an earlier rite. The family knew they would be subject to a substantial fine, but preferred to be penalized by government rather than risk divine displeasure. Understanding the seriousness of fear of the gods is essential to understanding Clark's drama.

From the foregoing it is clear that marriage, sex, and childbirth are matters of great social concern in life as in Clark's plays. Village life is far from private. Inappropriate behavior is seen as having effects far beyond the individuals who directly participate in such behavior. Even so inadvertent a case as that of a husband whose wives die is dangerous. After losing two wives, a man has little hope, if any, of securing a third. It is obvious to all that he is cursed. A child conceived incestuously, like Tufa in Clark's <u>The Masquerade</u>, or conceived under wrong circumstances, or born to an uncircumcised mother, is itself cursed and may be said to have little prospect of success, within the community at least, should it survive.

Most marriages and births are, of course, regular, and the processes of family life involve little concern for evil. Leis deals with these processes at length, but gives comparatively little attention to the important matter (here at least) of the development of narrative art through storytelling. He does describe the process, one that is reflected in Clark's vision of the Ozidi saga. A common story form begins with the call, <u>Egberiyo</u>, to which others present reply, <u>Ya</u>! This formula is used also to interrupt the story at moments of unusual pleasure. Tales commonly begin, "Once in Edo"--that is, Benin, the fabulous locale that stands in the same relation to Ijo narrative that Rome does to the "romance" of northern Europe. The Benin of such tales is no more realistic than the Rome of Shakespeare's Cymbeline.

Leis goes on to provide something of an aesthetic for the narratives. First of all, the story must be "true." That is, the narrator must attest to the accuracy of the tale and identify the source. With authentication, the story can be fabulous, heroic, or trivial and still be "true." Next, narratives often involve successive crimes, raising the aesthetic question of how guilt can be determined and the story resolved satisfactorily in terms of reward and punishment. Here a significant difference from the European aesthetic appears: guilt resides in the first wrongful act only. The perpetrator of that act is guilty. Other crimes that follow upon the first act are, in one sense or another, contingent upon it. This corresponds to Clark's finding that versions of the Ozidi tale provide no retribution for wrongs done by Ozidi. (Clark inserts retribution, however; this is discussed in chapter 4.) Leis notes, also, that numbers are important: three is most common, but seven is prominent as well. Seven, not surprisingly then, is the number of days or nights that are required for the performance or recitation of Ozidi's story. When the story is done, whatever the length, the teller calls out Egberifa! and the audience responds, Ya!

Ugo provides details of particular folktales to illustrate Clark's use of them in plays. Tortoise is the quintessential folktale character. He is the "trickster," familiar to every child in southern Nigeria. He corresponds to the Spider in Hausa tales and to Rabbit in the southeastern United States. One typical tale concerns the tug-of-war contests that Tortoise arranges between himself and Hippopotamus and, simultaneously, between himself and Elephant. Tortoise has no intention of competing, of course: Hippopotamus and Elephant pull against each other, each thinking his adversary is Tortoise. Clark glancingly uses this in Ozidi, when Ewiri-Tortoise tells Ozidi and Tebesonoma separately that each has challenged the other when, in fact, neither has done so. In an accretion to the same tale, Elephant in rage pursues Tortoise, who takes refuge below a huge cotton tree. When Elephant grabs Tortoise's legs, the trickster taunts his captor, saying he is pulling on roots, not legs. So Elephant drops the legs and pulls on roots. As Ugo says, Ofe in Ozidi works the same deception, and Ibobo in The Raft alludes to the story (10).

Ugo also observes that the base plot of Clark's The Masquerade derives from a common story of the girl who refuses all suitors until she is attracted to a monster in disguise. The usual end to such stories is that the monster is prevented from eating the girl (or whatever other terrible fate) by a heroic hunter who rescues her. Essentially, the tale is a caution to young girls that they should accept parental guidance in choosing a husband.

Riddles are an important part of Ijo folklore, and they play an important role in Clark's rhetoric, both in poems and plays. Much of Clark's poetic "indirection," though used in mature conversation (11), is based upon riddle. In Song of a Goat the masseur accuses Zifa of neglecting his wife:

> You have allowed the piece of fertile
> Ground made over to you to run fallow
> With elephant grass.
>
> (Goat, 6)

Ewiri in Ozidi warns murderers that their victim's son has come seeking vengeance:

> Many years ago several
> Of you here present planted a champion yam.
> Well, that yam you sowed several seasons gone by
> Has now grown beyond arm's span.

He calls this "our little conundrum," and, when it is not understood, he solves it himself (Ozidi, 64). This is an elaborate stylization of the playful children's riddle of the conventional sort: what is a child asleep in a house with no door? Answer, an egg. Ugo notes that riddles are essential to conversation and not confined to children's entertainment.

Children's songs are as common among the Ijo as among other people. Ugo quotes several songs that Clark recapitulates in English in plays. For example,

he opens the last movement of The Raft with Kengide
holding up his left hand with fingers spread. He tells
(not sings) a story.

> It began like this. The small fellow right outside
> Here happened one day to cry hunger. "Let's
> Go out and grab ourselves something," suggested
> His closest friend . . .

The story goes on until the thumb refuses to join in
the theft (Raft, 119). As Ugo reports the song, the
fingers and the thumb sing the following lines successively:

> Boda womu furu (Let's go and steal)
> Furu teki mie ngo (Steal for what?)
> Furu kumo (Don't steal)
> Woni sowei ngimi (We shall hide)
> Ari suogha (I am not with you)

Both the similarity and difference are apparent. Earlier in The Raft Ogro sings, imitating the engine sound of a "Niger Company" riverboat,

> "Lokoja's too far,
> "Lokoja's too far,
> But over there lie riches"
>   (Raft, 116)

This is spiritually akin to the lines Ugo remembers
from his childhood as the song imagined to be sung by
the stern-wheeled steamships on the river:

> Forcados--Burutu--One pound ten
> Forcados--Burutu--One pound ten

Just as Lokoja is the distant upstream point at the
Niger-Benue confluence, so Burutu and Forcados are the
coastal estuary destinations of the downstream river
traffic.

    Naturally adults sing, too. Ugo cites an Urhobo
song sung by women (like Clark's grandmother perhaps)
when returning home by canoe. Though not translated,
it is, Ugo says, "a form of prayer so that they will
arrive at their destination":

> Ewhe whe ro ko
> Eh, eh eh
> Ewhe whe ro ko
> Eh, eh eh
> Tsakpa avwovwe
> Terurun

This is clearly akin to Ogro's song

> "Good for nothing craft
> Hee hee!
> Good for nothing craft
> Hee hee!
> Just take me to port
> Safely!"
>   (Raft, 99)

A song of lumbermen quoted by Ugo underlines the significance of this industry to the Ijo and shows that bringing log rafts to the river and to the coastal ports, as The Raft, is often hard labor:

> Singer: Bei kpo ma tefereya?
>   (What type of work is this?)
> Chorus: Mie ngiyofa (There is no choice)
> Singer: Timba fere ton bakamo
>   (Lumber work weakens sex)
> Chorus: Mie--ngiyofa (There is no choice)

Such songs--especially the children's and women's songs cited--are reminders of the central proposition regarding Ijo life: it is lived in, on, and near the creeks and rivers. It is a water-borne life. The tides and the floods govern life. The ebb tide and dry season alike signify withdrawal, privation, or death, while the flood invites new growth and, optimistically, anticipates birth. Yet at the same time, in paradox, the excess of flood or tide can be disaster to people living as the Ijo do at the margin of land and water. It is tempting to base a philosophic principle on this paradox and apply it to Clark's works. His drama and poetry are both celebratory and pessimistic. His drama is paradoxical, whether heroic or tragic. The mood of Clark's work, overall, is ironic, as if his themes, like the tides, were subject to change, to mood, and to paradox.

Nigeria

The discussion thus far has dealt with Clark's homeland in a local way, but as was said at the start Clark is Nigerian. He cannot be treated as simply an Ijọ writer, however much he has drawn subject matter, theme, and imagery from the Niger delta. He left the delta after finishing secondary school in 1954 and returned to it upon retirement as Professor at the University of Lagos in 1980, but for the twenty-six years between he returned there only occasionally. Like two elder brothers, he entered the mainstream of Nigerian affairs. His work in many ways was influenced by his participation in Nigeria, the nation.

In 1954, independence from Great Britain was already assured within foreseeable years, though the eventual date--October 1960--was uncertain. Clark's formative years were those of post-World War II, a war that provided Nigerians with new ways of looking at their colonial position. The Atlantic Charter assured, in vague terms, "self-determination" for all peoples. England's Winston Churchill did not perhaps have Africans in mind when he agreed to the Charter, but Africans certainly applied the principles to themselves. A result was an impetus that led to the wholesale liquidation of the British Empire.

The war itself carried Africans far from home, into military campaigns in many lands, most famously Burma, where Africans learned to question colonial assumptions. The sacred character of the white man, for example, had enormous credibility until veterans of service abroad reported that white men were merely men--laborers, farmers, soldiers, as able to do menial work and to be wounded and killed as any others were. It is a remarkable factor in colonial history that the myth of white superiority maintained its credibility for so long.

The myth is a reminder of Nigeria's transformation over the last 150 years. In 1830 only rare and lucky visitors from Europe survived a journey inland. Far from the coast, the inhabitants of the hinterland conducted their affairs with little conscious reference to Europe. Then from 1850 the effectiveness of quinine as a prophylactic against malaria created a wholly new situation. European traders began, often at the point of a gun, to bypass coastal middlemen. Gradually a race for territories and markets with French and German rivals led the British to assert "protection" over the rivers, and a series of agreements among European powers between 1884 and 1899 effectively divided up the entire continent. Among the territories that Britain claimed was the one named (in 1898) "Nigeria." For the next twenty years, swiftly at first and with general success, the colonial rule was extended, defined, and made absolute. It remained firm, in spite of occasional troubles, until World War II and the consequent pressure toward independence. When independence came, petroleum was still a relatively small part of the Nigerian economy. But it rose in significance rapidly, and many believe that oil wealth played a profound role in the crisis, civil war, and military rule of the 1960s and 1970s.

Clark finished secondary school in 1954 and went immediately to a clerk's position at the edge of power in Nigeria. His post was in the office of Secretary to the Government of Nigeria. Though his stay there was brief--he entered the university within the year--the sophistication with which he would deal with public affairs was well prepared for. Nigeria's first constitutional election had taken place at year's end 1951-1952. In 1954 a new constitution deprived the central authority of general control over legislation and indeed created something close to three Nigerias--the West (including much of the delta), the East (with the remainder of the delta), and the North. For Clark, his brief period as a clerk in a strategic government office at a time of intensely rising African participation in government was important. He had already shown a precocious interest in literature (even attempting two novels in secondary school). That he should be intensely aware of colonial governmental processes just then doubtless contributed to such poems of protest against the colonial heritage as "Ivbie," which was completed only a few years later.

A third constitution of the 1950s was completed in 1958, with elections scheduled for 1959 and independence set for October 1, 1960. Thus the independence proceedings coincided with Clark's years at University College, Ibadan. He concluded his studies there in the final term of 1960, a few short months before independence. It is at least a reasonable hypothesis that the onset of political independence was a motivating factor

toward creativity at the university. New journals
inspired by the clan, by poetry, or by politics mush-
roomed, and Clark was among the enterprising editors.
The Student Union was highly political and Clark was a
leader of it, along with others who would play important roles in the crises to come.

The 1959 election stirred the hopes of the young
intellectuals for a new Nigeria. It neither satisfied
those hopes nor fully denied them. The three con-
testing parties were regional in appeal. The one that
secured the most votes was the most frankly regional--
the Northern People's Congress (NPC). Philosophically
it was the most conservative; it least welcomed change
and even had resisted the imposition of independence
before the North was thought to be prepared. (Education by Christian missionaries had been blocked in the
Islamic North, so the cadre of potential administrators
in the North was small, meaning that unwelcome southern-
ers were to be given authority.) The NPC aligned
itself, to establish a working majority, with the
National Council of Nigerian Citizens (NCNC), a party
strong in the East with considerable support in the
western delta. The third party, the Action Group, was
the opposition. Its strength was largely among the
Yoruba in the West. Although both the NCNC and the
Action Group had taken relatively radical positions
under colonial administration, when independence was
assured electoral politics inclined both parties toward
placating special interests. Thus while optimists
might hope for a new social and political order after
October 1, 1960, European and American observers were
inclined to applaud the stability that conservative
rule promised. For a time the observers from abroad
continued to applaud, while the domestic radicals came
increasingly to regret the failure of their dreams.

The sad history of 1960-1966 needs no recapitulation here. The climactic crisis is dealt with below in
the chapter on Clark's Casualties (12). From the
catastrophe a changed nation has emerged. Its continuing problems and the question of the will to solve them
are subjects of Clark's most recent poems, State of
the Union.

Clark's Nigeria

Clark's Nigeria is a mixture of the old and the new.

Unlike Chinua Achebe, who in his novels creates a point of view that is time-specific, Clark's plays and many of his poems represent a continuation of the past in the present. Ozidi, for example, is played with one actor as both hero and narrator. The narrator exists in time present, a time of national politics and motorcars. Ozidi is himself legendary--yet at the end Ozidi-and-narrator lead a single triumphant procession in which legendary and present time are blended.

Song of a Goat and The Masquerade are, it is true, made time-specific (recent) by allusions to the contemporary world, but their actions seem to take place in villages barely changed by recent history. In modern Nigeria there are indeed many such places, yet choosing them for his setting creates a temporal ambiguity that well suits his purpose, which is the evocation of traditional life, in much the same way that William Butler Yeats and John M. Synge sought out the old Irish mood--and sometimes tale--in a contemporary setting.

So, to, in the poems. "The Imprisonment of Obatala" is an evocation of Yoruba myth, similar in conception to Yeats's re-creations of Irish hero tales. Like Yeats and W. H. Auden before him, Clark chose his subject through the inspiration of a picture. The variety and complexity of Nigerian life, partaking as it does of the European as well as African cultures, are Clark's source.

This variety and complexity are Clark's own. He was "early sequester'd from my tribe" (13), but his connections to Kiagbodo were never broken. Being part of two worlds is the Nigerian experience continuing today.

One world is the English-speaking world. Many contemporary Africans deplore, and many others resent, dependence upon the colonial language. Clark had embraced it. Yet paradoxically he has used the colonial language as a defense against colonial degradation of the African world. For him the two worlds interpenetrate. They are not antithetical, but exist, develop, and change. English is essential to Nigerian nationality in Clark's view; he is frankly a nationalist.

His marriage confirms a nationalistic point of view. Ebun Odutola, when Clark first met her, was a beautiful young woman and talented actress beginning her academic career as an assistant lecturer in the new University of Ibadan School of Drama. Her origins were Yoruba, so the common language they spoke was the colonial language that is at the same time the national language. As an Ijo̱ man Clark was perhaps readier than most Nigerians to marry outside his clan. After all, most Kiagbodo men are bilingual, and Clark's own maternal grandfather, Amakashe Adomi, had an Urhobo wife, Clark's grandmother. Tradition in many areas of Nigeria requires marriage outside the paternal lineage but even so marriage is not thought suitable outside the ring of villages and towns where a distinct dialect is spoken. Yet Kiagbodo tradition permits both <u>kie-ere</u> marriage such as that of Clark's mother, Poro, to his father, Chief Clark Fuludu Bekederemo, and <u>bra-ere</u>, in which the bride may not even speak the local language. Thus Clark in marriage blended the old Nigerian traditions of his home with the new forms of a cosmopolitan English-speaking society. It is a society neither Ijo̱ nor Yoruba, not Igbo or Hausa, but Nigerian.

Nigerian too are the poet-playwright's elder brothers, lawyer-politician Edwin Kiagbodo Clark and diplomat B. Akporode Clark. That three sons of the same parents should be ranked among Nigeria's foremost citizens is surely a tribute to the imagination and vision of their parents. In 1941, when time had come for young Clark to begin school, there was no satisfactory school for him to attend at Kiagbodo. War had halted the spread of government schools. Miles down the Forcados River, opposite the old Royal Niger Company island port Ganagana, at Okrika (also called Ofonibengha), the Nigerian Native Administration had earlier established an excellent school. Clark's chieftain father chose to pay the school fees and provide support for these sons, among his many children. Clark recalls his own uncertainty when his father personally handed him over to a distant family connection, a chief who assured the father that the boy would not come to harm. It was the start of a twenty-year pilgrimage toward honor and distinction.

One event at that school led to Clark's creation of the play <u>Ozidi</u> and re-creation of the <u>Saga</u>. That event was the recitation to enraptured school children of the story of Ozidi. The storyteller was Afoluwa of Ofonibengha. Many years later, Clark's schoolmaster, Thomas Onduku, who had invited Afoluwa to tell the story, collaborated with Clark in setting down the Ijo̱ version of the <u>Saga</u>.

Later, Clark's father moved him nearer home, to Jeremi, to prepare for secondary school. The best secondary school in the delta—one of the best in West Africa—was Government College, Ughelli, to which Clark passed after some months at Jeremi in 1948. Clark spent six years at Ughelli, during which time he seems to have read all the books in the school library. Cyril Carter, English teacher, house master, and school principal, gave the boy access to his own personal library, including the regular monthly contributions of the Readers' Union. By the time Clark completed examinations for the Cambridge School Leaving Certificate, he was so well prepared and ambitious that he had attempted to write novels. In a year, after his clerkship with the Government Secretary, he went on to University College, Ibadan. During his Ibadan years he showed the most precocious talent that West African literary history had yet seen.

The remainder of Clark's career, as it is traced in chapters to come in this volume, can be summarized briefly. After taking his degree in 1960, he became an Information Officer with the Ministry of Information at Ibadan. He left this post to become editorial and features writer for the Express newspapers in Lagos. His reputation as a rising young journalist recommended him to the Parvin Fellowship program at Princeton University. He spent most of the academic year 1962-63 in the United States as a Parvin Fellow, with results discussed at some length in chapter 3.

Upon his return to Nigeria, he began his professional academic career. He first accepted a Research Fellowship at the University of Ibadan, in which position he investigated the Ozidi tale, discussed below in chapter 4. In 1964 he joined the staff of the University of Lagos English Department. Later (1972) he was appointed Professor. While at Lagos he composed Casualties (see chapter 5), poems reflecting the crisis and civil war of the late 1960s. Aside from a year at Connecticut Wesleyan University (as Visiting Distinguished Fellow), Clark remained at Lagos until 1979. He spent a year on study leave at Ibadan prior to retirement from his position at Lagos in 1980.

He now lives and writes at his home near Kiagbodo, when he is not occupied with the PEC Repertory Theatre that he and his wife have established in Lagos.

Chapter Two
The Ibadan Years

J. P. Clark's career as a poet began while he was an undergraduate at University College, Ibadan. Many, if not indeed all, of the poems published in his first volume, Poems (1), 1961, and also his first play, Song of a Goat (2), published later the same year, were written before Clark took up journalism as a writer for the Express newspapers in Lagos. This chapter will discuss these first two major publications. Together they show a prodigious talent awakening and growing strong and confident. A final section to this chapter will examine briefly Clark's early journalism and fiction.

Poems

Many of Clark's earlier poems were published in student journals, particularly the Horn and the Beacon. The Horn was to some extent Clark's own creation; he was its founding editor. The Beacon was the publication of the student association. It was printed rather handsomely, in contrast to the Horn, which was cyclostyled (or, in American usage, mimeographed). Some of the journal poems have never been republished. Others were printed in Poems virtually unchanged. A few show Clark's development at its early stages and are of special interest. In the discussion of the journal poems, it will be assumed that they were written earlier than the poems or versions published in Poems, though in fact there is no evidence for this other than priority of publication.

On page 6 of the first issue of the Horn (probably early in the 1957-58 academic year) there is an untitled poem, "My head fills out in fear." It anticipates Clark's liberal use of imagery from his childhood in the delta, and it also shows, in rudimentary form, the most basic pattern of Clark's early poetry. Finally, it suggests the disquiet that pervades Clark's poetry, an anxiety that energizes the commonplace (3).

The basic pattern is occasional; a feeling elicits a comment on the feeling:

> My head fills out in fear
> The relic of many a tender year
> Spent bailing bilge for grandmother
> In her dugout on the Niger;

The obvious infelicity of years "spent bailing bilge" may account for the suppression of the poem. The next lines satisfactorily explain the "fear":

> When from midstream at night
> I behold dark clouds of trees in flight,
> Drifting past upon the ceaseless shores,
> Take on weird shapes and force:

The remainder of the poem identifies the frightful images, oil palms like "wizards, plumed out in eagle, / Intent on who next to kill," and other trees like "massive . . . matrons" or "monsters in snoring repose . . . All huddled on the water's edge."

With this may be compared "For Granny (From Hospital)," one of Clark's best-known poems, a version of which was published in the Beacon's second issue as well as in Poems (4). It, too, is occasional, but the fear has a cause: Clark is ill and the fear is of death as he addresses the same grandmother alluded to in the earlier poem:

> Tell me, before the ferryman's return,
> What was that stirred within your soul,
> One night fifteen floods today,
> When upon a dugout
> Mid pilgrim lettuce on the Niger,
> You with a start strained me to breast:

The present fear of the ferryman (to the land of the dead) has reawakened the old fear he felt fifteen years ago (when Clark was perhaps six years old) (5), when "Granny" seized him suddenly. The image of the dugout is repeated, and the pilgrim lettuce (which a note, in A Reed in the Tide, identifies as a weed that floats in the Niger flood) invokes both the river and a sense of spiritual purpose, making a more interesting image than any in the suppressed poem.

In both poems, the colon is followed by examples,

but only in "For Granny" do the examples expand the reader's consciousness beyond the river experience and its immediate anxieties. In "For Granny" the first example asks if "the raucous voice / Of yesterday's rain" evoked in her "the loud note of quarrels / And endless dark nights of intrigue / In Father's house of many wives?" The second is more powerfully imagistic and calls up a cosmic fear embodied in the river's reflection of the stars:

> Or was it wonder at those footless stars
> Who in their long translucent fall
> Make shallow silten floors
> Beyond the pale of muddy waters
> Appear more plumbless than the skies?

The new "wonder" transforms Clark's grandmother into an archetypal observer, losing reality in awesome appearance. Instead of the mere anxiety of "My head fills out in fear," arising from a closely similar physical situation, "For Granny" shows something more akin to awe.

In Clark's early poetry, the three factors--structure based upon occasion, imagery drawn from the river (or from mythology), and heightened fear or dissatisfaction--recur. Sometimes the "occasion" is only a photograph, and often the water-related imagery combines with other kinds, but the troubled mind that is revealed in the poems persists. "Grief, chaos, insecurity, and irredeemable loss," Romanus N. Egudu has said accurately, "are the hallmarks" of Clark's early poetry (6).

The <u>Horn</u>'s third issue (there were four, all under Clark's editorship, during academic 1957-58) contains another poem that he later suppressed, "The Cry of Birth" (<u>Poems</u>, 15; not subsequently reprinted). It is both more painful and more admirable than "My head fills out in fear." The occasion is "An echo of childhood" that rolls "back into brilliant memory / the anguished cry of my birth; / . . . a voice . . . [I] thought to have shed with infancy, / returns." This voice evokes, "by reflex horror / an instant glimpse--the guilt of all our see:" ("all" is omitted in the <u>Poems</u> version), this last word a punning anticipation of "the sea" whose "echo of despair and stress / precedes me like a shade to the horizon."

Between "see" and "sea," the images are derivative

from English poetry of the nineteenth century, a
mélange of impressions from Wordsworth, Tennyson, and
Arnold, with a key image from Greek, rather than Ijo,
mythology.

> Ah, the souls of men are immersed in stupor
> who, tenants upon the wild isle unblest,
> sleep on; oblivious of its loud nightmare
> whose treacherous motions bedevil our breast.
>
> But all night, through its long reaches and black
> I wander as Io, driven by strange passions,
> within and out, and for gadfly have, alack,
> one harrowing shriek of pain and factions-- (7)

The alien tone and the vagueness of the sea as a local
image mark the poem as more European than African, but
a compelling quality emerges from the borrowed verse:
it is ambition. Clark, though no more than a second-
year student, has dared to link his own voice with his
models' and has managed to express something of his own
lyric anguish, different from theirs. It is as if he
chose to use recollected themes not merely because he
lacked other poetic material (though surely that lack
was a problem) but primarily because the alien themes
suited his alien mood. The poem, though not a success
for a mature poet, is striking in a young one and is a
strong indication that Clark had at the time the arrogance to dare writing poetry that invited, even challenged, criticism. Indeed he would swiftly go farther
and challenge England itself using the techniques of
England's poets.

The challenge was published in the second number of
the second volume of the Horn, and dated "28.X.58."
(Abiola Irele had succeeded Clark as editor.) The
title was Ivbie, and with it the young poet established a claim to be of the first rank among African
writers. The poem inevitably was a sensation. No
Nigerian had published (perhaps none had written) a
poem of such substantial length, well beyond lyric
effusion. Further, while a variety of more-or-less
anticolonial or proindependence polemical poems were
regularly appearing, few had merit as literature.
Ivbie was clearly a poem that would last beyond its
occasion. The editor called it "a very special poem"
in a "special issue" and said that he hoped "it will

The Ibadan Years

contribute to that spirit of 'Negritude'" championed by Clark while he was editor. Also the editor hoped the poem would "receive the serious attention it deserves." He was not disappointed.

The first response, in the next number of the Horn, was a negative commentary by Obiajunwa Wali, who found parts admirable but the whole inartistic and a failure. The Beacon, however, responded in May (1959) with republication of the poem; this time it was printed rather than mimeographed and the quality of production was clearly superior. Ivbie had, as it were, graduated from ephemeral publication into permanence (8). Clark had stunned the Ibadan world--small world though it was then--with a work of sustained magnitude. And Clark was still at the time only an undergraduate.

Wali's commentary was clearly an attempt to moderate the popular enthusiasm for Ivbie. That enthusiasm was no doubt excessive. Clark's achievement was precocious but not the product of artistic maturity. Yet in 1958 independence for Nigeria was only two years away, and the anticipation of the great time to come increased a local passion for African achievement, a passion for the celebration of things African. Ivbie is both a celebration of Africa and an attack on colonialism. Clark could deal with the European, could challenge the European, and could do both in the European's own language, using the techniques of the admired T. S. Eliot.

Clark thus early adopted Eliot's aphorism (from his essay on Philip Massinger), "Immature poets imitate; mature poets steal," taking lines or styles where he found them and endeavoring at least to make them his own. Not only in Ivbie, of course: Hopkins, for example, seems barely present in this poem, but is deliberately imitated in "Ibadan Dawn" (subtitle "after Pied Beauty") and in at least two "Variations on Hopkins" in Poems (pp. 39-40), "On the Theme of Child Wonder" and "On Faith." Blake's influence is obvious in a line from "The Tyger" lurking in Ivbie, when motorcars blaze (rather than burn) in "the forests of the night." Usually, however, Clark internalizes his borrowings from English tradition, again following Eliot: "The good poet welds his theft into a whole of feeling which is unique; the bad poet throws it into something which has no cohesion." Clark, as in using the line from "The Tyger," sometimes falls into the latter category. Yet the clear errors are rare, even in so early a poem as Ivbie.

Eliot's The Wasteland is so obvious an influence that one need only remark that it accounts for the multiple voices in the poem, the abrupt juxtapositions, the use of a divine speaker, the marginal annotations, the use of literary tradition (Blake, Burns, Coleridge, Conrad, Lawrence, Orwell, and others, perhaps even Lyly), and the perception of the contemporary experience as a muddled contrast to an implied ideal. This use of artistic tradition is entirely legitimate, and the poem succeeds or fails not because of Eliot but because of what Clark has done with the material he used. Clark's use of Eliot to attack the colonial influence is an inherently successful irony: it was the Britain of The Wasteland that claimed superiority over the Africa Britain violated.

Ivbie is an Urhobo word that may be taken to mean (in Clark's words) "The wrong done to you without any hope of justice." From that delta word, so glossed, the poem springs.

It begins by asking, in what turns out to be irony,

> Is it not now late in the day,
> Late, late, altogether late,
> Turning our doubled backs upon fate,
> To pluck out of honey fresh milk fangs?

The question answers itself: yes, it is indeed late. But "fresh milk fangs" carries the threat of what is to come. In a new Africa, it is late but not too late, and that is what matters. Ivbie is very much a poem prompted by the new national consciousness. It is "negritudist" in impulse, a fact that requires a brief explanation.

Negritude, as all students of modern African literature know, is a literary philosophy that celebrates blackness in a generalized belief that Africans have, in their racial or cultural being, special characteristics which Europeans lack. When Clark initiated the Horn he identified negritude with the "perhaps . . . sentimental and moonish" idea of "the dark Africa, careless of sputniks and missiles, and enjoying the earlier wise direction of her ancient rulers, teachers, and prophets." "Westernization," he went on, is kill-

The Ibadan Years

ing "that sense of deep calm and flow, mystery and rhythm which for ages has been [Africa's] peculiar grace." The <u>Horn</u>, he said in this first-issue editorial, is founded to combat the West's "subtle imperialism."

<u>Ivbie</u> was written when these ideas were near or at the center of Clark's creative impulse. The poem is not too late precisely because its anticolonialism is (or seemed at the time) in the process of realization through political liberation. The transition from colonial violation to African serenity concludes the poem. Clark addresses the West:

> Pass on in mad headlong flight
> O pass on, your ears right
> Full of throttle sound,
> So winding up your kaleidoscope
> Leave behind unhaunted
> An innocent in sleep of the ages.

Europe is departing, and <u>Ivbie</u> is a celebration of that fact.

At the same time it is a warning to Africa. Clark does not mistake independence for a return simply to the old ways. He is conscious (again in the <u>Horn</u>'s inaugural editorial) that he and his fellow intellectuals cannot use their African languages; the colonial transformation is "for the time being" a profound difficulty. But knowing the injustice, seeing it clearly, may help to purge the worst effects and restore some measure of negritudist innocence. Such seems to be Clark's belief at the time.

<u>Ivbie: A song of wrong</u> is a poem in five "movements." The first accuses the European strangers of wrecking "With alien care and impunity" both land and belief. The strangers are both concerned and callous, contemptuous

> "Lice, lice, my dear, may infest
> Stately woman's crest."

and amazed

> <u>Rare works of art discovered in</u>
> <u>Tin Mines! Another in Benin</u>
> . . . .

> Treasures, so many and beautiful,
> Bartholomew Diaz and Sir John
> Hawkins, wondering adrift on
> A log ferry boat,
> Did not know, Cellini
> Dwelt among cannibals

These mixed feelings are the product of ignorance augmented by arrogance. To contrast with the colonial responses, Clark reminds the reader

> In the shadow of all trees
> Lie holy unravelled dust

and he urges, "Seek out the shrines of Ifa"--the oracle of the Yoruba people--and then recalls a legendary African king as a reminder that great and even terrible events occurred without European guidance.

The second movement briefly observes that Africa was "unguarded" against the invasion, an invasion of immense implications. The exploitation is compared (both literally and figuratively) to the rape of African women by European men:

> The dark flesh rudely torn
> And grafted on to red fetid sore
> Breeding a hybrid lot
> To work the land of sunset.

In an attempt at "restitution" a symbolic white woman, "Sweet Mrs. Gamp, not a coward," joined her husband, but with a terrible result--an abomination. She

> Delivered amid cries in the mission ward
> A wisdom-toothed child.

(A note on the abomination is found in *A Reed in the Tide*, 39.) Mrs. Gamp and her abominable offspring lead directly to the imposition of the European religion,

> Is it truce or ruse
> That peace which passeth all understanding
> O big brother in heaven!

European civilization and its paradoxical effects are the subjects of the third movement. In vicious irony, Clark demands to know where the light is that Europe told itself it was to bring to pierce the imagined African dark? The only visible sign is automobiles, "Austin Herefords" going "toot"

> Blazing wide trails of gold
> Through the forests of the night.

From this point, the poem changes. The specific indictment of the colonials is complete. Now, in the fourth movement, Clark'e eye turns inward. What were the gods doing?

> Say, you communal gods at the gate
> Has that whiff of carrion crept
> Past your bars as you slept?

To this, a mythic Mother replies, urging her children in, to safety.

> An unlaid ghost
> Has come into the village
> Tonight out of the coast
> I hear his wings flapping in the twigs

The Mother becomes the supreme deity Oyin, woman and mother (also called the high god Tamara), who cares for her children, providing the rainbow to lead the fearful home from the dangerous bush. Oyin delivers the key warning that is at the heart of the poem:

> Fear him, children, O fear the stranger
> That comes upon you
> When fowls have gone to roost.

And

> O fear the dragon smoke-cloud
> That hangs bloated, floating over
> Roof-thatch mangoes and lime.

The image shifts to the snake-bird fallen early in the market

> Digging with his bristle fangs
> Open communal graves amid confused clangs
> Of race and riot

Fear the poison passed out or spat
Straight on our ancestral seat

The poison, "dissolving, will deluge all the earth."
But this warning of Oyin, who has become at the end of the movement an owl, was not heard but rather feared:

I the white bearded woman
Of night fame saw all
But men heeded not my hooting
Placed instead penalty in warning
And finality in brief omen.

So it was that the first generation to meet the strangers failed. How, the fifth movement seems to ask, has this present generation succeeded? It has not succeeded: "more white than white,"

At the office desk, we clapped ourselves on the back;
So well-fed on sweet quotations and wine
Were we, with pride, we said:
"Forget O forget . . . to forgive is divine."

For the speaker of the poem, that is not enough. "Yet in my father's house I cannot sleep." The house here is the ancestral house, and in it the present generation cannot rest though drugged with the colonial comfort as the earlier generations had allowed themselves to be drugged with colonial gin. The sleeplessness of the fifth movement is extended through thoughts of faith, of suicide, of indecision (like Hamlet's or the uncertainty of the Niger whirlpools), of the sense that the speaker himself is now Oyin's enemy and that She must protect her children from him too. He is without certainty or place:

I cannot sleep nor act
And here I pace her bastard child,
A top twirling out of complexity
"Gnawing at my finger-tips deep perplexity."

The poet as Oyin's "bastard child" is a central concept in Clark's poetry. Although the concept is complex, the essential idea is clear enough: the African who has assimilated European culture is beyond reassimilation into the culture of his fathers, while he still is not separated enough to be other than African. The bastard child is no one's child and the identity he achieves is something new, something ambiguous and uncertain.

Ambiguous but not necessarily lost. In the final movement the bastard child can address the colonial world from his father's house:

> I,
> Reared here on a cow-dung floor,
> From antediluvian shore
> Heard all, and what good it did!
> "Magnificent obsession" now magic chords
>   are broken!

The negritudist way is open now, now (in 1958) when the British soon must withdraw. They will, in the final lines of the poem (quoted earlier), pass on. Implicit is the speaker's belief that Africa, once free, can be in time "unhaunted."

The romantic hope that concludes the poem is not an aberration. Although grief or even anguish marks the poem as a whole, the negritudist philosophy requires intellectual passivity--"An innocent in sleep of the ages"--as a counter to Europeanization. In the first movement Clark used rhetorical questioning to deny Europeans the understanding intrinsic to African life, an understanding based on physical rather than intellectual being:

> How can they in the fixity
> And delirium of a glance
> How can they catch the thousand intricacies
> Tucked away in crannies
> And corners perhaps known only to rats?
> Cast away in the heat of desire
> The shifts hanging in the wind
> Now groins want oiling?
> The sanctuary of things human is swathed
> In menstrual rags, not in the market place.

Africa's "sanctuary of things human" is denied by Mrs. Gamp's fastidiousness, which creates only abomination. Innocence is radically different in Africa from the false sexual purity of post-Eden Judeo-Christian morality in which innocent and shameful verge on being synonyms. The young poet rejects his own mission education lest he too be unable to "catch the thousand intricacies."

The conclusion is in keeping, too, with an odd optimism that occasionally breaks through Clark's pessimism and irony. It occurs at the end of Clark's Casualties, when Clark foresees a better time coming after the tragic events of the 1960s, and it is further developed in the beautiful and often anthologized "Night Rain," which was first published in Poems. It is appropriate to discuss it in this section of the chapter because its publication in Ibadan (74 [September 1962]) shows that it was intended for journal publication but subjected to delay.

"Night Rain" might almost be a companion-piece to Ivbie. It is, save for the commonality of endings, wholly in contrast. The locale is indigenous to Clark's childhood and seems more an evocation of that time than an expression of time present, after the deculturation process of education has brought into being the bastard child. The home with its thatch roof is by contemporary standards an impoverished one, but there is in the poem neither complaint nor regret. Rather, Clark's language is an idealization of rain, comforting rather than threatening: rain falls

> through sheaves slit open
> To lightning and rafters
> I cannot quite make out overhead
> Great water drops are dribbling
> Falling like orange or mango
> Fruits showered forth in the wind

This is quickly mitigated by a metaphor (that comes closest in the poem to suggesting a world beyond the delta), followed by the comfort of maternal presence:

> Or perhaps I should say so
> Much like beads I could in prayer tell
> Them on a string as they break
> In wooden bowls and earthenware
> Mother is busy now deploying
> About our roomlet and floor.

The mother secures the time, place, and circumstance

with "her practical step" as she moves stored goods

> Out of the run of water
> That like ants filing out of the wood
> Will scatter and gain possession
> Of the floor.

With quiet economy Clark then elevates the circumstance to a universalizing calm:

> Do not tremble then
> But turn, brothers, turn upon your side
> Of the loosening mats
> To where the others lie.

The rain has created a magic spell that removes the danger even of owls or bats, leading to the poem's resolution:

> So let us roll over on our back
> And again roll to the beat
> Of drumming over all the land
> And under its ample soothing hand
> Joined to that of the sea
> We will settle to a sleep of the
>   innocent and free.

"Night Rain," with its perfect rhythms and patient observation of life well lived in the manner of the people, is an ideal negritudist poem. No other of Clark's poems matches its tenderness, for tenderness is not characteristic of Clark's poetry. A few other poems do, however, share the negritudist impulse rather clearly, most notably "Abiku," which was published around the same time in Black Orpheus 10. "Abiku" is also a remarkably successful poem both in content and structure. Because of its clear structure it is a useful poem to discuss as a transition to the remaining poems published in Clark's first volume.

Clark's "Abiku" has not been well served by comparisons with Wole Soyinka's admirable poem of the same title. Soyinka has some privilege, it is true, because abiku is a Yoruba word, not an Ijo, but Soyinka's poetic mode is tangential, Clark's is direct, so the comparisons are more useful as student exercises than as criticism. Abiku is the child, known to virtually all southern Nigerian societies, who perversely dies, frustrating his parent, and then returns and returns, to die and to die again.

Clark's poem is composed of six sentences addressed to the errant child. They progress from a gently ironic suggestion that the <u>abiku</u> "stay out on the baobab tree," to an equally gentle denigration of the parent's home, "it leaks through the thatch . . . bats and owls . . . tear in at night . . . the bamboo walls / Are ready tinder," which completes the first phase of the poem. The poem makes its turn with the tentative transition "Still" to start the third sentence, which mildly praises the family's endurance:

> Still, it's been the healthy stock
> To several fingers, to many more will be
> Who reach the sun.

Then the poet firmly invites the spirit-child:

> No longer then bestride the threshold
> But step in and stay
> For good.

A sentence reminds the child it is recognized by the scars and notches given during previous incarnations. Then a final sentence plays upon the human sympathy of the still only part-human visitor:

> Then step in, step in and stay
> For her body is tired,
> Tired, her milk going sour
> Where many more mouths gladden the heart.

The empathetic simplicity of the poem is its most appealing quality. Unusually, Clark has taken a grief-laden circumstance and deflected the grief. The sentiment is so mildly understated that it engages the emotions without cloying. In this poem, as in most of his best poems, simplicity and understatement create poetic experience.

An ideal example of simplicity and understatement, this time used to define an inexpressible sorrow, is "Streamside Exchange," which must be quoted in its entirety.

> Child: River bird, river bird,
> Sitting all day long
> On hook over grass,
> River bird, river bird,
> Sing to me a song
> Of all that pass
> And say,
> Will mother come back today?
>
> Bird: You cannot know
> And should not bother;
> Tide and market come and go
> And so has your mother.

It has almost observational detachment. With irony recalling William Blake, Clark internalizes the two roles: the hopeful boy and the mocking, fatalistic bird.

More overtly personal in its opening, but actually less so in total effect, is another widely admired poem, "Fulani Cattle." Originally published in the Bug, another student journal, in 1957, the poem arises from a familiar sight on major roads in southern Nigeria, droves of cattle herded to market on the coast from hundreds of miles to the north. The sight awakens a melancholy guilt in the poet:

> Contrition twines me like a snake
> Each time I come upon the wake
> Of your clan,
> Undulating along in agony,
> Your face a stool for mystery:

Their stoicism in suffering on the way to slaughter suggests to the poet a creation that, as in Blake's "The Tyger," frames the character created:

> Can it be in the forging
> Of your gnarled and crooked horn
> You'd experienced passions far stronger
> Than storms which brim up the Niger?

On the other hand, the slaughter may be welcome:

> Or likely the drunken journey

> From desert, through grass and forest,
> To the hungry towns by the sea
> Does call at last for rest.

That the poem is early Clark shows in the lame ending, in which the poet asks the animal to "reveal . . . the patience flowing from your tail"; it is lame because the flow is poorly imaged, and the cow's revelation of anything at all would negate the rest of the poem.

More personal is "Agbor Dancer" (Horn 3, no. 1 [1959]), though its first fifteen lines are an objective but delightful description of an image "caught in the throb of a drum,"

> In trance she treads the intricate
> Pattern rippling crest after crest
> To meet the green clouds of the forest.

The final stanza recalls the "bastard child" of Ivbie:

> Could I, early sequestered from my tribe,
> Free a lead-tethered scribe
> I should answer her communal call
> Lose myself in her warm caress
> Intervolving earth, sky and flesh.

Though the poem implies no deeply felt emotion, it makes clear that the young poet was recurrently troubled by the loss of his traditional upbringing, with a continuing intellectual perplexity. The problem is given a sort of resolution, though without an African context, in "Horoscope," in which the "bastard child," addressed by that name, is told that if the moon pulls tides in good scientific understanding, then surely the vaster stars control "man, this clot / Of clay, three quarters diluted in water."

There is little question that Clark is at his best in poems where the poet's relation to the subject is more ambiguous than in "Horoscope" and "Agbor Dancer." Very personal or anecdotal poems--"Tree" or "Ring Round the Moon," neither of which has been reprinted since Poems--tend to be weaker still. Also weak are the merely observational, descriptive poems, even when they are experimental, like his imitations of Hopkins. One of them, "Ibadan Dawn," is rather better than the others. One important reason is its happy evocation of

The Ibadan Years

a delta bride at her wedding, "blushing calm from flush of cam, / Morning comes breathing flowers, warm and light . . ." to represent the city coming alive.

"The Imprisonment of Obatala" is more interesting than the Hopkins imitations though it is, like them, experimental and impressionistic. The poem gains clarity if one has seen the photographs published in <u>Black Orpheus</u> of a batik by Suzanne Wenger having the same title. The photographs, and Ulli Beier's notes on the Obatala legend, are clearly Clark's inspiration. As described by Sangodare Akanji, the ten-by-fourteen-foot cloth batik has "a dark, near black background" on which "the drawing is carried out in a very pale yellowish green and the ornament and some of the larger shapes are indigo and a reddish brown," each color varying in shade.

> A sweeping movement descends through the long arms of the creator god Obatala who is looking down from the sky . . . a minor motion surging up . . . seems to sweep right through the body of the woman worshipper who supports the central figure, that of Ajagemo, the high priest of Obatala.

Ajagemo is reenacting the imprisonment of the god.

> Above him one of the two leopards of Sonponna the god of suffering links up with the huge figure of . . . Obatala. Finally Sango the god of thunder rises . . . holding the lightning in his hand. The . . . sun, containing . . . interlocked snakes . . . forms a calm centre . . . there is [in a corner] the white elephant . . . the baobab tree, home of the spirit children [cf. "Abiku"]; and Eshu, the god of fate on horseback. (9)

Clark in the poem calls attention to the elongation of the limbs of figures, particularly Obatala:

> Those stick-insect figures! they rock the dance
> Of snakes, dart after Him daddy-long arms
> Tangle their loping strides to mangrove stance,

as they interact. He notices the colors too,

> One leap upon the charcoal-coloured ass

Swishing ochre urine toward palace and sun,

but the key to reading the poem is found in the legend to which Clark alludes. Obatala, god of all creation, was tricked by Eshu so that when Obatala captured Sango's stolen horse, Obatala was imprisoned seven years for the theft. Crops and mothers alike failed until Sango discovered the error, and then the world was saved. As Clark says, concluding the poem,

But the cry of a child at what it knows not
Evokes trebly there the droop, mud-crack and clot.

The legend is Yoruba; this poem like "Abiku" arises from Yourba inspiration. Both poems use delta imagery--thatch, bats, owls, and mangrove (though only the last is found only in salt swamps and creeks).

Overall, the collection Poems is uneven, as a collection published when the poet is newly out of the university would be at best. What is remarkable is the enduring merit of so many of the poems. Clark tried a wonderful variety of styles and had some success with most. His form--the mode for his styles--seems to have evolved less consciously than the experiments would suggest, perhaps being more a result of a characteristic state of mind than conscious intent. The mind is clear, sensitive, more than a little ironic, and above all, aware of the grief of living.

Song of a Goat

The title of Clark's first play, the one-act Song of a Goat, has two origins. The play has its climax around the ritual sacrifice of a goat; thus the title is to be taken literally. On the other hand, the title is a translation of the Greek words tragos, "goat," and oide, "song." These are generally thought to be roots of the word "tragedy"; thus the title is a pun. The pun calls attention to the idea that classical Greece and modern Ijo share a blood ritualism that is largely absent from contemporary European cultures. The title is then an assertion of the legitimacy of African tragedy, an assertion that though the form be alien in origin, its use in Africa is natural and appropriate.

Structurally, the play is almost a classic tragedy.

The hero, Zifa, is a man of substance in his community but bears the twofold burden of a family curse and sexual impotence. His aunt Orukorere anticipates the tragic consequence, but her gift of prophecy (given by the sea gods) has the same limitation as Tiresias's and Cassandra's: she is not believed. Zifa's wife, Ebiere, takes as her lover Zifa's younger brother Tonye. After she has become pregnant (a departure from classic tradition allows the time to pass), Zifa discovers the infidelity. In proud rage, he ritually slaughters a goat and requires Tonye to put the head into a pot too small for it, symbolically indicating his brother and his wife and their illicit relationship. Tonye hangs himself and Ebiere collapses. Zifa departs and a neighbor (as Messenger) describes his suicidal walk into the sea. The neighbors serve a choruslike function and the Masseur who opens the play (and in one version closes it) serves much the same function as the choral leader in classic tragedy.

Though formally Song of a Goat resembles Greek tragedy, its less obvious antecedents are more modern. Among the many cultural activities at University College, Ibadan, during Clark's last years, there were performances of plays by John Millington Synge and William Butler Yeats. Also the English Department offered a special paper on Yeats. Clark was in the group (10). Synge and Yeats would both have interested Clark, who was seeking in his poetry to deal with traditional life, as was pointed out earlier in this chapter.

Synge, far more than Yeats, dealt with the commonality of people in his Irish plays. He showed that rural folk could be shown both comically as in In the Shadow of the Glen and tragically as in Riders to the Sea. Further, he showed that humble folk may have great dignity. Clark felt that the Ijo̱ people, too, should be depicted with dignity.

Yeats wrote plays drawn from Irish folklore. Because few of his characters were contemporary rural folk, Yeats's language, unlike Synge's Irish colloquial style, was elevated poetic diction. The example of an heroic play verging on tragedy like On Baile's Strand could well have urged Clark's competitive muse to compose a play of about the same length (most of Yeats's plays are one act long) on an African theme. While there is no evidence to show that On Baile's

Strand directly inspired Clark, the correspondences between the plays are suggestive.

Both plays use choral groups (kings and neighbors) very lightly individualized by lines of dialogue. In both the violence (Cuchulain's killing of his son; Tonye's suicide) takes place off stage. In each the hero is drowned in the sea and the fact is reported, not shown. Yeats's play opens and closes with characters who are not essential to the action (a Blind Man and a Fool); Clark's Masseur opens the play (in a highly relevant conversation) and closes the play (in an alternative ending). Most striking is that in each play the hero's grief results from the death of a close blood relative.

Both plays use vigorous but elevated diction, though Clark's diction uses figures that are far from Yeats's style, and it is this diction that best individualizes his dramatic art from these suggested influences--for Clark has created an English-language dramatic rhetoric to represent Ijo rather than English (or, in Yeats, Irish) culture. It is a poetic mode quite different from anything in Poems; its closest literary analogy is the parable-aphorism as Shakespeare used it. Gloucester's "As flies to wanton boys, are we to th' gods, They kill us for their sport" (Lear 4.1. 36-37) is a memorable example with which may be compared Clark's lines explaining why Ebiere has "grown very queer of late." "Bring up a chicken among hawks / And if she is not eaten she will eat." The Masseur's observation about Ebiere's womb at the start of the play is similar.

>An empty house, my daughter, is a thing
>Of danger. If men will not live in it
>Bats or grass will, and that is enough
>Signal for worse things to come in.

A difference is apparent immediately: the house image is extended well beyond Shakespeare's characteristic mode (Shakespeare's extended metaphors usually become very complex in their imagery; his aphorisms, like Clark's hawk-hen lines, are brief). Indeed, Clark continues the house image in the dialogue that follows (Ebiere's response is first):

>--It is not my fault. I keep my house
>Open by night and day

> But my lord will not come in.
> --Why? Who bans him?
> --I do not hinder him. . . .
> My house has its door open I said

A few lines later the Masseur inquires further, "Has he a house elsewhere?" Ebiere's "No" completes use of the image; Zifa's impotence has been established by indirection.

This indirection is closely akin to the Ijo riddle. As was observed in the first chapter of this book, the riddle is a verbal entertainment throughout Ijoland (and indeed much of the entire world; in most of Europe and America, however, riddles are treated as stale jokes). Clark shows how the riddle can play an active role in communication of ideas too sensitive for direct speech. When the Masseur must talk with Zifa about his impotence, he introduces the subject with a riddle, which Zifa quickly understands:

> --. . . You have allowed the piece of fertile
> Ground made over to you to run fallow
> With elephant grass.
> --What do you mean?
> --Anyone can see the ears and tassels of
> The grass from afar off.
> --Has she told you something?

Zifa defends his secrecy with another riddle: "Shall I show myself a pond drained dry . . . ?"

The lines among metaphors, riddles, aphorisms, and parables are often hard to draw. A contrast of Clark and Yeats may be helpful in distinguishing the first two. The opening lines of Yeats's *The Only Jealousy of Emer* are an extended metaphor (simile):

> A woman's beauty is like a white
> Frail bird, like a white sea-bird alone
> At daybreak after a stormy night
> Between two furrows upon the ploughed land . . .

The metaphor is extended into the question, asked twice, what time and circumstance could bring into being such "loveliness." A figure such as this is very rare in Yeats's plays, while extended figures are common in Clark's. Yeats's rare figures are little poems in themselves, while Clark's are to the point, dramatically direct. That is, they are dramatically direct while being rhetorically indirect. Sometimes the audience can understand a riddle when the character cannot, as when the Masseur urges Zifa to allow his brother to assume the husband's duty: "One learns to do without the masks he can / No longer wear. They pass on to those behind."

The riddling mode of metaphor enables Clark to keep his dramatic dialogue constant in its allusion to the circumstances and mode of life in the delta. Song of a Goat as a result escapes the absurdity that might attach, in some audiences, to hearing native speakers of African languages conversing about their own affairs in the king's (or the queen's) English. Clark has succeeded in indigenizing English to his purpose, making the standard language represent an African reality. This is not done through a translation of Ijo speech into English, but rather through "finding the verbal equivalent" in speech which will represent characters "in their original and native context," to quote Clark's own observation on his method (Example of Shakespeare, 92; see 93 for comment on "indirection" in Song of a Goat).

Clark's taste is not faultless. Wilfred Cartey provides an excellent and admiring analysis of the correspondences between images and feeling in the play, but he also notes occasional contrivances that seem less natural than Clark's better figures (11). What, however, is remarkable is that Clark's first play should show firm rhetorical control, a clear and original rhetorical objective of verbal equivalence that is clearly conceived and persistently adhered to.

Performances of a play are the tests of its dramatic effectiveness. As a play for the stage Song of a Goat has had a mixed history. Robert G. Armstrong has commented on the Mbari Club production at Ibadan (apparently the first production, with Clark's own participation in planning), which he found to be very bad. The worst single thing about it was the untheatrical public slaughter of a real goat, a catastrophic action that could only make the rest of the play anticlimactic (12). Una Maclean like Armstrong disliked the alternate ending used (13), but Armstrong's comment that the Masseur was shrieking at the end strongly suggests that bad acting contributed to audience disapproval. Molly M. Mahood shared the general conviction that cutting the throat of a goat on stage was a serious error (14). Nkem Nwankwo in Horizon (1, no. 2 [1952]) suggested that the Mbari Club was unsuitable for play production; that fact may have made the performance less successful than it might have been. Olga Adeniyi Jones as Ebiere nearly struck a spectator with firewood, creating unintended comedy, and Wole Soyinka (the dramatist; then director of the performing group, the 1960 Masks) adopted a "sullen mixed-up-kid stance." The Masseur's final speech was "an epitaph on the disaster." The reviewer's one markedly favorable comment was on Francesca Pereira as Orukorere; she was "most impressive." Since Orukorere is a complex role, the effectiveness of the actress in an otherwise weak performance says clearly that Clark's dramatic conception of that role at least was sound.

Cyprian Ekwensi reviewing a later performance at the Commonwealth Arts Festival found Francis Akeru "impressive" as the Masseur in a generally slow production (15). Scott Kennedy's New York production seems to have gone very well; a Ghanaian performance, however, seems to have achieved only absurdity (16). Other productions, of which there have been many over the years, affirm that the play has substantial dramatic interest and effectiveness, and is not "closet drama." The lack of sustained commercial production, on the other hand, implies the not-surprising idea that Clark's first play has limited audience appeal for the great theatrical centers of England and America.

Cultural misunderstanding may account partly for the play's limited success overseas. The roles of the Masseur and Orukorere are apt to be misunderstood, and the curse that underlies Zifa'a impotence is not clearly developed in the text but must be guessed at from hints. Impotence itself and its social significance (as distinct from the personal problem) are apt to be poorly understood beyond Clark's home regions. Also, traditional means of coping with impotence may be surprising or even shocking.

The Masseur, as was pointed out in the first chapter, is an important person in an Ijo community. He is called upon when women fail to bear children. It is assumed that the woman's internal organs are improperly arranged; the "pusher" feels out the fault and massages the woman's body correctively. His successes and failures are easily observed, so he must take pride in his work and preserve his reputation. As Clark's Masseur says, he will not take fees and agree to help merely to keep up appearances for Zifa. "What, are people to understand she failed / To respond even to the touch of my fingers?" (Song, 8).

Additionally, the Masseur is a natural confidante. Like a small-town family physician, he knows the secrets of the community and keeps them well. He reminds Zifa that in all the years since he and Zifa's father were youths together, "I have not shared / A man's secret with another." Indeed, Zifa's father being dead, the Masseur stands in loco parentis: "I helped to bring [you] into this world / And [your] fortunes I should love to watch / As a father his sons." This closeness at the start of the play accounts probably for the alternate ending which brings the Masseur back on stage--an alternative perhaps asked for by the acting company, who felt a need both for a philosophic note to conclude the play and for the parental figure to sound it.

Orukorere, who ends the play in the main text, is limited by her obsessive state of mind from appearing either philosophic or parental. She is partially mad because she is one of those women who are said to have been chosen by the sea divinity. Such women refuse marriage, though they are very desirable, or if they do marry, their husbands suffer the jealousy of the sea (Elechi Amadi's novel The Concubine centers on the latter sort of woman; Orukorere is the former). All such women suffer in one way or another because of their intimacy with the god. Orukorere rejected the oracle's divination (probably, that she was sea-chosen) and for that was given "double vision" together with the fate that she would not be believed (Song, 18).

Orukorere is, rather confusingly, called "mother" by Zifa and by his son Dode, while Dode calls Ebiere by her given name. This is especially confusing to the reader when both women are near. In the following dialogue Dode acknowledges his mother's gift of a dragonfly, then tries to tell her about his great aunt:

> --Ooo! how bright his colours! But Ebiere, Mother, mother, she's been--
> --All right, all right, Dode, I quite follow. Your mother's been drunk again . . .
> (Song, 19)

It is a case of there being no correspondence between English and Ijo̱ usage; "mother" is the only satisfactory English substitute for the variety of meanings in the Ijo̱ word--but a substitute, not an equivalent.

The family curse is rather more difficult to understand because Clark is vague about its antecedents. Orukorere's father is clearly implicated: a neighbor implies that he would knowingly kill clansmen--a terrible sin--and would be indifferent to the fate of a son-in-law married to his sea-beloved daughter:

> --She will have no man for a husband
> Why, young men came from all over the land
> To ask her hand of her father.
> --They all got it from him, you cannot
> Doubt that. He would as easy kill inside the
> Clan as outside it.
>
> (Song, 18)

But the scope of the play limits tracing the curse. Whatever its cause, the curse has been reinforced since it originally affected Orukorere and her brother. She became bride of the sea; he (Zifa's father) died of leprosy. The latter provoked Zifa's crime against the gods.

> My father who they dared
> Not spit at when he lived is dead
> And lying in the evil grove.

The townspeople required that the abomination be removed from the town and disposed of in the traditional land reserved for evil spirits. Zifa's loyalty required that his father's spirit continue to participate in the communal life:

> Of course, I have recalled
> Him unto town so at times of festival he can
> Have sacrifice.
>
> (Song, 9)

The Masseur mildly observes that Zifa may have done so "a little bit early," but Zifa shows that the community in its traditional wisdom recoiled angrily. He says,

> And for that they have picked my flesh

> To the bones like fish a floating corpse.
> Others grumble it was in time
> Of flood.
>
> (Song, 10)

The townspeople know that the gods do not forgive without compensation, and no indication appears that any member of the family has a willingness to propitiate. Zifa, in particular, defies tradition not only in regard to his father's second burial but later on in the ceremony of the goat. This point will be returned to in a moment.

The curse is the apparent cause of Zifa's impotence. Impotence has great social significance in societies where children are major proofs of a man's substance, wealth, and prestige. Economically, children augment the labor supply in the family. Also the increase in potential labor carries with it social rewards. Children further promise the ancestors future sacrifice and thus enhance the spiritual life of the community. Failure to produce children robs the living and the dead of their increase and their honor. Infertile wives are held in contempt; infertility is presumed to be the woman's failure. Male impotence upsets the social order and lies outside the presumed order of nature.

Children are so necessary that the impotent man will usually find a surrogate to father his children, since the children of his wives are part of his own household. A trusted friend might serve; a younger brother is suggested to Ebiere by the Masseur: "That'll be a retying / Of knots, not a breaking or loosening / Of them." The assumption of the role might, however, be unacceptable to the ancestors, so a ceremonial propitiation of them would be required. The Masseur explains this to the distressed wife:

> I understand
> Your feelings, understand them very well. But
> You are young still as I say, and do not
> Know the ways of our land. Blood of a goat
> So large a cowrie may pass thro' its nose,
> A big gourd of palm wine and three heads of
> Kola-nut split before the dead of
> The land, and the deed is done.
>
> (Song, 5)

The solution is, unfortunately in the event, rejected by Zifa, while Ebiere accepts the younger brother without ceremonially appeasing the ancestors.

The ceremonial sacrifice of a goat, when it occurs, is a parody of propitiation. Zifa for years has neglected the gods, in spite of Orukorere's urgings. Then, upon discovering that Ebiere is pregnant by Tonye, he proposes a sacrifice without prior ritual cleansing. Orukorere warns him,

> But you are
> As yet not cleansed, and for that matter all
> The concession is reeking with rot and
> Corruption.

Zifa, in reply, perverts her meaning:

> In that case, it needs drastic
> Cleansing which is what we shall now all perform.

Orukorere, frightened, warns him again, and adds an aphorism:

> Be careful, son, and do nothing that is
> Rash. When the gods ask for blood it is
> Foolish to offer them oil.

Again he perverts her meaning and proceeds rashly to slaughter the goat, scattering blood which, he says, "should cleanse the compound / Of all corruption today." He has, however, one ironic "little detail" before beginning "In real earnest." The "detail" is requiring Tonye to put the goat's head into too small a pot. When the pot breaks, the symbolism of Tonye's adultery is complete, and the "real earnest" sacrifice --Zifa's murder of Tonye--can proceed (<u>Song</u>, 36-37).

The murder of a kinsman is the most terrible crime of all among the Ijọ, and Zifa's sacrifice of the goat was a defiling sacrifice, not a cleansing, because its function was as prelude to the worst of abominations. Zifa has insulted the gods and defied the clan. These are new crimes beyond his previous neglect of the gods and beyond his impiety in bringing his father's spirit too soon back to the community. An Oedipus of the delta creeks, he has let his pride govern his life in defiance of the will of the gods.

It remains only for him to discover his folly and be led by that discovery to despair.

This is, in classic tragic manner, what does occur. Tonye's suicide is itself an abomination but it is heroic. After the mad slaughter of the goat, Tonye accepts the fact that he will die. His choice is to be killed by his own brother or to kill himself. One or the other must then be guilty of a terrible crime. Tonye chooses to be guilty and to spare Zifa the crime of murder. As Zifa says, after discovering the hanging body, "The poor, brave boy has truly done for me" (Song, 40). Tonye's courage in suicide is, not at all ironically, "a brotherly act," like keeping what Zifa "was powerless to keep / In the house" (Song, 41). Zifa's speech of guilt after discovering the body should not be read as irony. It is confession and tribute.

Zifa then gives himself to the sea. It is an appropriate end to his despair, for among the Ijo (and especially within Zifa's family) the gods of the sea are central to life and death. The audience needs to understand that Tonye must, like his father, go to the evil grove for burial. Zifa, spared the abomination of murder, chooses to die in the sea. First he calls to a steamboat (such as he himself piloted) that he will not come to the ship "today." Though his death may be called suicide, Clark implies something more positive. One neighbor says Zifa "waded into the deep / As one again in sleep," and another neighbor attests that the end

>   was so like
> A dream at flood time it was
> Impossible to hold at anything.
>   (Song, 44)

Zifa's death is more a final yielding to the gods whom he so long resisted, than yet another crime against them.

The alternative ending, though it seems to have been an afterthought, is functional in that it deals with an important final question: Who should be blamed? (In the first chapter it was pointed out that Ijo tradition holds the first guilt as ultimate.) Orukorere indirectly accuses the Masseur, and then implies that it no longer matters:

>   Others have made off

> With the wares you put a price
> On. But now all that is over and
> Only the laughter of wind fills out
> In my ears.

The Masseur, when she has gone, accepts the accusation. He tells the Neighbors,

> No doubt,
> There are some, as she said, among you
> Who will say it is I started it all.

He agrees that he sought to quench the "fire," but denies he set it:

> This was not fire begun
> By ordinary hand. All fire comes
> From God, else why the thunder?

And he concludes that seeking a solution to the complex of causes is as futile as understanding life itself. Echoing King Lear, he warns

> Do not, my people, venture overmuch
> Else in unravelling the knot, you
> Entangle yourselves. It is enough
> You know now that each day we live
> Hints at why we cried out at birth.
> (Song, 48)

At the end of Clark's play, the community, Deinogbo, survives the loss and continues. The people have learned to bear their own lives perhaps more stoically after the example of the fall of Zifa's household. What will happen to Ebiere, Dode, and Orukorere is unclear. It is thought Ebiere suffered miscarriage (Song, 42), but it appears in The Masquerade, to be discussed in the next chapter, that Ebiere died, not the child (Masquerade, 68). Clark may not have planned the sequel play, which was written (or at least finished) in the United States. Clearly, however, he saw that the family he had created, like the great houses of Greek tragedy, was too rich a mine to be abandoned.

Fiction and Journalism

Clark's first juvenile interest as a writer was in

fiction; in secondary school he began, but did not finish, two novels. There is no evidence, however, that fiction continued to interest him much. Nevertheless, he published at least two stories, one of them apparently while he was still a student, the other in 1964. Between the two, he was a journalist with the Express newspapers in Lagos, attended Princeton University and wrote a journalistic account of the experience (see next chapter), and began his career as an academician.

One of the two stories is unavailable. It was published apparently in a Sunday journal and titled "At the Waterfront." It was, a critic has said, "successful" using "the fantastic and the mysterious" rather than ordinary life (17). The fact that Clark sought no subsequent publication suggests that such favorable comment did not improve his own judgment of the story.

The other story appeared in Amber and soon after in Black Orpheus (18). Titled "A Stop in the Night," the story is a dialog encounter between a European woman and an African man. The woman confesses to an abortion and the man is dismayed only at the price she paid. The irony is neat. The attempt at brittle, social conversation is not effective. The opening lines of the story, however, show Clark's imagistic skill:

> The sky, spliced as between a pair of scissors, falls in one vast, voluminous fold of night. . . . Blindly, over wet weeds soaking through to my socks, I part my way up the drive to where a one-room flat squats smiling uncertainly by a bush no longer so primeval.

The preparation for a dubious occasion is fine; the occasion is not up to its preparation.

Like his fiction, Clark's journalism began at the university. He appears in the fourth issue of the Beacon (May 1958) as theater critic (a production of Mozart's The Magic Flute) and as memorialist (a co-authored piece on a gifted teacher). He continued writing theater criticism occasionally when working for the Express, but his most interesting journalism was the feature writing he did for the Daily Express (19).

In a two-part piece, Clark recounted his search at Badagry, near Lagos, for the first two-story building in West Africa, and then described a similar investigation of the even older slave chains that survive from the days when Badagry was an important center for the trade. The articles are light in tone, and sometimes mildly ironic, as when Clark baits an old woman by asking how much her father asked as the price of a man. "It was a male affair," she answers, turning Clark's irony onto himself. In another report, Clark admirably details "The maze that leads to the Osha throne," a complex competition, rooted in tradition and history, for the chieftaincy of Onitsha, eastern Nigeria's great trade center.

The signed articles do not show if Clark was an effective journalist. Very little of his work was signed, so it is in the anonymous columns of the Express that his mark was made. Clark used his journalistic experience only once later, because his resignation from the Express in 1962 was final. His one later journalistic effort was America, Their America (20), an account of his Parvin year, the subject of chapter 3.

Chapter Three
Clark's Parvin Year

In mid-1962 J. P. Clark resigned his position as features and editorial writer for the Express (Lagos) newspaper in order to accept appointment as a Parvin Fellow at Princeton University in the United States. Clark later wrote a book about that year, America, Their America (1964, 1968). It is an antagonistic report on both the University and the United States. The antagonism is in part a reflection of the fact that, a few weeks before the fellowship was to end as planned, it was abruptly terminated and Clark was ordered to return promptly to Nigeria. Although the account is sour, it reveals that Clark's Parvin year was a dynamic one and decisively affected his life and art.

The single most dramatic fact is that Clark's journalistic career ended. Why the end was permanent is problematic, but the reason may be connected with another obvious fact. This second fact is that during the Parvin year, Clark resumed the writing of plays and poems. The Masquerade and The Raft were written in America, and the new poems in A Reed in the Tide date from the period. He had apparently suspended--perhaps abandoned--serious literature when he joined the Express staff.

Some less obvious results of the Parvin year for Clark are changes in his approach to art. These less obvious results are dependent upon the ending of his newspaper career and the resumption of serious writing, yet they are also in a larger sense more significant. These subtler changes are a new sense of the theater and its possibilities, a more intense concern for African, particularly for Ijo, tradition, and aesthetic acceptance of politicization of art. If these changes did indeed take place, then America, Their America takes on added interest, transcending its rather limited literary appeal.

This chapter will take up, first, Clark's book about the year, although it was written after his return to

Nigeria. Then this chapter will deal with the plays Clark wrote in America. Finally, it will take up the volume of selected poems, A Reed in the Tide, with attention to the new poems from the Parvin year.

America, Their America

America, His America. The book must first be examined for what it is superficially. It has two rather distinct aspects, though these are frequently intermixed: first, a narrative of a personal experience, and second, a commentary on the United States and its culture. The latter aspect was for Clark the more significant one, as the title implies. Yet for some readers at least the distortion glass of the personal experience seems to control the observation of America. For that reason, the present account will deal with the personal experience first.

The book opens, artistically enough, with the end. Clark and his friends, four Americans and one Nigerian (Chinua Achebe, the novelist), are seen at New York's international airport in late May (the year is 1963, though Clark never says so). In a few moments, on the next page, Clark departs for London, en route to Lagos (leaving, inconsequentially, his overcoat behind). Then swiftly the narrative reverts to "not quite a year before"--nine months or less--and identifies an initial unpleasantness at the immigration desk upon Clark's arrival in the United States. One of the officials "hit me across the shoulder, quite viciously" (America, 17). This astonishing treatment, like many other incidents in the book, is not so inexplicable as the language Clark uses to describe it. The official was cordially welcoming the visitor and congratulating him on his Princeton University fellowship.

Clark's persistent identification of well-intended words and actions with their opposite marks the personal narrative as jaded at best and more probably perverse. The odd part is that Clark seems at times to take pains to show how courteous and patient the people who offended him were. In the present instance, he not only records the official's words of welcome, but also the expert advice, about taxis and trains, extraordinarily and freely offered. Other examples of Clark's initial prejudice immediately follow. The large automobile in which a Nigerian diplomat carries him to New

York City is, although admittedly of ordinary local size, "ostentatious . . . as only politicians and their conmen can afford" in Nigeria. When the diplomat reminds Clark that he is in the United States,"It was a reminder I was to hear rubbed into me again and again like salt over a sore for several months to come" (America, 18). The origin of the "sore" is obscure; Clark seems to have had it before the airplane landed. Again perversely, he says he is unsurprised by the steel and glass structures of the city, "But what struck me immediately was the dust and smut covering the face of New York" (America, 18). With such a beginning, it will not be expected that America will delight the newcomer. It rarely does.

In discussing Clark's attitudes the present writer must acknowledge that he was (a little before the time Clark was there) sa student at Princeton University, that he holds two degrees from that institution and that he was by choice a resident of the town for more than six years. In America, Their America the people mentioned include one of this writer's friends, as well as a close relative, a mentor, and others whom he knows less intimately (1). As a result he can empathize better with the Princetonians than with Clark. Also he is more sympathetic to Princeton's manners than Clark is, and he may be inclined to some impatience with Clark's behavior. This prejudice, if that is what it is, may distort the literary criticism somewhat. But it should immediately be added that America, Their America is no great object as literature. It is essentially journalism, and subject therefore to journalistic rather than literary strictures.

Clark was late arriving at Princeton, and remarks with irony that it was a "great misdemeanour" to miss "some tea party or other" honoring the Parvin fellows (America, 27-28). The delay was the result of the same sort of discourteous self-indulgence that marked his entire Parvin year: he has a subsequent invitation elsewhere that he preferred to accept.

In Clark's defense it must be said that misunderstanding on both sides is probable. There is no doubt Clark was confused at first about what was expected of him. It is also true that he clung to his misapprehensions, and may have done so deliberately. He describes his final conversation, near the end of the academic year, with the head of Princeton's Political Science department. Clark knew that he had no examinations to take, but said anyway, "even if I regarded myself as a regular student, that should not remove my right to skip classes and pay for it at exams" (America, 207)-- a "right" he enjoyed at University College, Ibadan. Minutes later, he asked the director of the Parvin program "whether the occasional absence from classes made one a delinquent student, especially where grades were not taken and no examinations were sat for" (America, 209). Clark half admits the contradictions in his own defense, but he disguises (in the word "occasional") his wholesale failure to attend seminars that, he says, "I had no nose or training for" (America, 206). In fact, as can only with difficulty be deduced from America, Their America, Clark took every possible advantage from the Parvin program, and avoided meeting any obligation that direct supervision did not impose on him. Even so, he managed to excuse himself from many meetings of the one seminar that was compulsory for all Parvin fellows (America, 206).

Another defense is attributable to misunderstanding on the part of the program director, Dr. Robert van de Velde. It is beyond question that the program staff saw Clark as a fiery Nigerian journalist, a man already prominent as a leader in the public affairs of his country. To van de Velde's surprise, Clark was more interested in poems and plays than in politics and newspapers.

The incapacity of the program to meet Clark's interests was remarked by an "old friend and expert from the State Department in Washington." He was responsible for evaluating, after personal interviews, the usefulness of the program to the participants (America, 222). The evaluator is not named by Clark; he is Donald Easum, and a portion of his report (which Clark never saw) reads, ". . . Clark might have contributed more to Princeton--and vice versa--had he been assigned an adviser from the Creative Arts Program. . . . They might have given up on him fairly early, but it could have been worth a try" (2). Obviously the Parvin director was unprepared for a Fellow who fitted no appropriate Parvin Fellowship category.

Substantial efforts were quite reasonably made to enrich Clark's experiences in American journalism. Van de Velde arranged visits to the central New Jersey newspaper (the Home News in New Brunswick) and to the nation's capitol's largest daily (the Washington Post). Both visits started well, yet each soured. Perhaps the reason was that Clark really did not care about newspapers, so it little mattered to him whether he was offended or offensive. In any case, Clark each time found occasion to be offended. At the New Jersey newspaper, the guilty remark was made by the promotion manager. Clark quotes him as saying of the local blacks, "We are doing a lot for them." Clark is dismayed. "Poor blacks," he thinks. "Like children or aliens, things are usually done for them" (America, 46). He finds himself offended, and quickly departs restraining himself from rudeness. In Washington, he engages in a restaurant shouting match over the character of India's Prime Minister Nehru (America, 52). Clark found no profit in either occasion. At least none is recorded.

The Parvin director, after learning about Clark's interests, arranged for him to investigate American theater as well. Clark credits van de Velde's help, yet he begins his report on the experience with a thoroughly odd account of a conversation with Alan Downer, a theatrically minded professor of English (America, 85-86). Clark, by his own account, never allowed the conversation to get under way. Downer committed the following errors: (1) he asked if Clark's play was written in English, (2) he was surprised that the play had been published, (3) he asked if publication (and perhaps performance) was in London, and (4) he asked if the play was comedy or tragedy, one act or longer. Clark rose; the professor rose; Clark departed. It is unfortunate that Downer was not better briefed by van de Velde; it is also unfortunate that Clark should have been so unhelpful. Treated with persistence and patience, Downer would surely have greatly enhanced Clark's American experience. Neither patience nor persistence is, however, a marked characteristic of Clark in America.

After the failure with the professor, van de Velde put Clark in touch with Mrs. McAneny, the general manager of Princeton's McCarter Theater, who, Clark says (in an implied contrast with Downer) "accepted me instantly and on equal terms" (America, 88). He got along with this lady very well; however he soon alienated the then-current McCarter stage director. He told that gentleman that the actress playing Antigone, "al-

though showing the timber necessary for her part, proved a rather wet affair, don't you think?" Understandably, the director declined to respond (America, 91). Clark shows a misanthropic innocence in reporting his own behavior.
Van de Velde later arranged for what was to prove a momentous experience at Washington's Arena Stage. The experience was certainly influential in Clark's later decision to adapt into English drama the festival drama Ozidi, and it may have influenced composition of The Raft, so it is of special interest here. "The proscenium or picture-frame stage," he says, "had . . . become the one image of the theater fixed in my mind" (America, 93). In contrast to that image, "The sheer architectural actuality of the Arena alone was overwhelming" (America, 94). What thrilled Clark was a splendid 30-by-36-foot stage, surrounded by four tiers of seats. One of these tiers was removable to permit three-sided staging rather than four. As Clark recognized at the time, this arrangement was similar to his childhood experience of village "festivals and performances at the town square or market place." The crucial difference was that the festivals had not influenced his conception of "theater." Clark does not say so, but it is evident that the "bastard child" phenomenon was again at work: the traditional performance did not seem to him "theater" until he legitimized it by overseas example. Later Clark would complain about Nigerians who "require the special aid of programme notes" to deal with theatrical practices unlike those taught in English schools (Example of Shakespeare, 96). Clark had learned his lesson in Washington.
Though the Parvin staff was helpful, Clark's own resourcefulness accounted for most of his contact with theater people. Before coming to America, Clark had begun angling for an American production of Song of a Goat. Indeed, a Madison Avenue (i.e., advertising industry) friend was planning for a production. Unfortunately (as Clark admits) Clark's unexpected antagonism cost him both the production and the friend. The friend, in obvious innocence, imagined that Song of a Goat should be performed by blacks. "And the impression," Clark replied, "would be that a play written by an African cannot be performed by white people. . . . We act Shakespeare at home" (America, 100). Clark's hair-trigger response to implicit racism precluded his

understanding his friend's interest in, not what was possible, but rather what would be popular. The first problem, as Clark's New York friends understood it, was to be assured of an audience and to give employment to black actors. In time Clark accepted the idea of a black production, and for a while had reason to hope for a mixed cast production. But both were too late. Song of a Goat did not then achieve performance on (or off) Broadway in New York.

Clark is oblique about his personal relations with the theater people whom he liked. His personal narrative, like the commentary, is largely limited to unpleasant encounters and critical observations. Even obliquely however he manages to show that there may be some justification for van de Velde's remark, "Clark was living in New York on Parvin money." Clark refers twice, rather casually, to "my lodgings down in Greenwich Village" in New York (America, 65, 103) and one may easily get the impression that Clark took the bus to Princeton primarily for once-a-week seminars. He was lonely at times in New York--he mentions a not uncommon "fruitless night of seeking for lasting warm contact" before boarding a morning bus to Princeton (America, 219)--but he does not dwell on loneliness any more than on happier feelings.

Whatever further adventures are significant to the personal narrative may be left to discussion of Clark's commentary on America--except, as a transition, Clark's reaction to the Cuban missile crisis. Before his arrival, Clark would not have known that in July of 1962 United States intelligence had reported that the Soviet Union had begun shipment of missiles to Cuba, and that by August 29 United States spy airplanes had confirmed that Soviet military construction had begun. However, on October 14, it was headline news for Clark and everyone else that a ballistic missile, evidently capable of reaching targets in the continental United States, was identified on its Cuban launching site. Clark was, with the rest of the world, witness to a period of intense anxiety that was climaxed by United States "quarantine" of Cuba (including the threat to board Soviet ships and remove weapons en route to Cuba). It was brought to an end by the Soviet decision, on October 28, to remove the missiles. Many believed that nuclear war was narrowly averted.

Clark has two accounts of his response. He told a

Washington Post luncheon group, "I slept quite soundly in the thick of the crisis" (America, 50). Later in the book however he mentions "those terrible days of tension" and then he recalls asking "the Colonel"--van de Velde--"And you have no plans to fly Parvin Fellows home?" Hearing a negative, Clark went on, "I think I better book myself a seat home on the next plane." He describes his words as "flippant" (America, 193), but van de Velde recalls having to persuade Clark not to leave immediately. In any case, Clark contradicts his own brag to the Post group. After the talk with van de Velde, Clark says, "I slept fitfully" through a nightmare vision of America insanely at war (America, 187-93).

America, Bad America. An America hurtling into nuclear holocaust over Cuban missiles was not the image the Parvin Fellows Program was designed to project on the minds of nine promising young leaders of developing nations. Rather, the program had a quite different idea, indeed only one idea, central to its purpose: that there is a special thing which, if known, would make America better understood abroad, that thing being "American democracy." Set against a bilateral U.S.-U.S.S.R. nuclear confrontation that threatened all life on earth, "American democracy" must have seemed paltry, even fraudulent in Princeton that autumn. It is beyond question that early weeks of the 1962-1963 academic year were gravely overshadowed by the threat of American power unchecked and unaffected by democratic processes. If Clark had not been skeptical before he came, he may easily have become so in October. Granted as well Clark's idiosyncratic behavior, and predictable responses to it, he was very likely to carry away an idea of a thoroughly bad America.

To encourage understanding of America, van de Velde conducted the one seminar required of all Parvin Fellows; meeting every Thursday afternoon, it was called "American Civilization." This course may have sought to be a corrective to Clark's "perennially sullen" (America, 121) attitude, but if so it had little success. In the chapter "The American Dream," Clark attacks the American "belief in the personal ownership of property." This, he seems to have concluded, is the commanding delusion of American society. Paradoxically, the evidence for this conclusion as well as the criticisms of the delusion seem both drawn from the seminar. Clark's solution, state capitalism, on the other hand seems drawn from his experience before Princeton. Workers, Clark told a cab driver in New York, in Ghana and Russia work "in state-owned plants." Why then should workers strike (as newspaper employees were doing in New York just then)? "You'd be killing the plant you pay yearly tax on," Clark concluded. The driver was confused (America, 127).

Another alleged delusion Clark mentions is that the United States, a "union of several disparate, self-repellant elements," should be expected to last. However, he admitted that "the gossip columnist" (Clark himself?) might overlook "some rock of convenience" that would keep the "marriage" intact (America, 133). The most severe internal division that Clark detected was between north and south "over the natural rights guaranteed the individual, black or white, by the American Constitution" (America, 132). It was an issue of considerable interest to Clark.

For an educated African, America had the deep fault of racism to start with, even before the threat of missiles. In 1962, after nearly a century of "freedom," blacks in America were still the objects of concern, pity, and contempt among the dominant white classes, and the complexities of race in America had long been publicized abroad. Not surprisingly, Clark sought out blacks in America in what may have been an attempt to understand them better. His chapter "The Blacks" is both personal narrative and commentary intertwined. It is as if the experience, however poorly understood, is the commentary--and the commentary is all Clark cares to reveal of the experience.

The commentary is disguised, in part, as experience. Clark has adopted, for example, a classic legend: "the major, if not the entire, source of light in the heart-breaking, bleak confines of the Negro in America [is] the matriarch" (America, 68). Two real people give substance to the legend. One is Gloria, a Columbia University student whom Clark had met while she was on a research trip to Nigeria. The other is Gloria's mother, called "Sister," a worker in a laundry plant (a "Jewish laundry plant," Clark for no clear reason specifies). Aside from Sister's cordial hospitality, she is wholly a textbook creation (a rather poetic textbook, of course, in Clark's version of the cliché):

> There she sat, the archetypal image of mother and
> mourner as well as guardian and co-sufferer of every
> member of her embattled race. For hundreds of years
> . . . she wept and waited; as all her sons were
> forced out into the fields to labour for others to
> reap the abundant fruit, and for this flogging and
> worse misfortune has been their wages; as her
> brothers were hurled out of the house to be hanged
> . . . ; as her daughters, desired and defiled by
> lustful masters, were made to bear a bastard breed
> . . . she has watched and waited in vain . . .
> (America, 70-71)

Except for the calumny "bastard breed"--reflection of a contempt for American blacks that the chapter sometimes shows--the whole passage might have been paraphrased from one of the books assigned by van de Velde in "American Civilization."

Clark divides American blacks into two groups, each exemplified by a cluster of experiences. One cluster he found at Princeton town, in "a house half-hidden . . . by shadowy elm trees," a house which proves to be a (private?) bar, busy with blacks. (They speak a patois known to no population group in America; Clark evidently neither visited them nor listened to them carefully.) Clark is treated pleasantly enough by these people, but his tactlessness (Clark admits it) alienates them. A reference to "Black Moslems" [sic] elicits "you pity us very much, don't you?" from a young man who has just bought the stranger a drink. An elderly woman (matriarch? Clark does not say) agrees, "it don't look you like our ways, least of all, our drinking and singing habits." Clark adds a suggestion that a revolution might be in order. "There he goes," a disgusted listener responds, "The fellow's come from Africa to do our fighting for us" (America, 63). The bar seems to be Clark's closest contact with working-class Americans (of any color).

The rest of black America is itself subdivided into (1) the middle-class blacks who are "much embarrassed that they stand out at all" and (2) the middle-class blacks who "make a profession of their identity, and indeed a booming business out of it" (America, 72-73). The former group merits only a contemptuous glance; the latter, largely identified with "the American Society for [sic] African culture," enjoys a rather full range of invective. They are accused of many faults (though few AMSAC members could certify Clark's accuracy): they exclude "even those whites with genuine interest and perhaps better knowledge of Africa"; they seek out pampered or wealthy blacks from abroad while removing themselves from "the bad breath and sweat of the man uptown in Harlem"; they "mix-up and masquerade" African artifacts and visitors, yet lack understanding and knowledge about African art, history, and geography; at a Christmas ball for African ambassadors, AMSAC leader Dr. John A. Davis led the United States Ambassador to the United Nations (Adlai Stevenson) to make a speech when he should have invited an African ambassador to speak; they fail to remember Pan-Africanists "Marcus Garvey and Dr. Du Bois"; they remember and admire each other, without discrimination, repeating platitudes and stereotypes about "Negro . . . soul"; they claim unlikely black achievements and admire black artists for the wrong reasons; the artists themselves are poor craftsmen, and deal only with "protest and prayer"; and, finally, they direct their bitterness against the whites, forgetting "the blackman's brother in Africa who sold him into slavery for a few tinsels and drink" (America, 74-83). There is probably deliberate irony in this last remark, made by a son of Kiagbodo.

It would be a mistake to conclude that Clark disliked all American blacks. He makes a notable exception in the case of "Sam Allen who really is the poet Paul Vessey [sic]" (America, 81), for example. Moreover, Clark managed to become friendly with a few of the people at the Princeton bar, whom he came to call (he says) "my folks of St. John's Street" (the street in fact is plain "John Street"). One couple included a former army captain, now an attendant at a women's club, and his wife, companion to a wealthy white female; together their income, Clark suggests, was better than many "college teachers and trained technicians" (America, 217).

Another couple shows the difficulty Clark had with black friends. This elderly pair invited him to dinner, to lend his prestige to the creation of "a community and holiday centre for the Negroes, just as the Jews and others do for their people." Clark neither accepted the invitation nor saw them again. In general, he says, it was better to avoid "my American Negro friends" lest they ask "me to do something or other to help them" (America, 218-19). Although Clark did not automatically dislike blacks, he did, it seems, generally avoid them.

Ignorance of Africa was disturbing to Clark when he discovered it in conversation with blacks; similar ignorance among whites, combined with experience of the Cuban missile crisis, must have seemed worse. It leads Clark to rhetorical enthusiasm: Americans are, he found, "So ignorant and almost fascist, so stay-at-home like a wall-gecko, and so conformist and scared" that Clark is incredulous. At, of all places, a meeting of the (international) "local Rotary Club," industry executives did not know where Nigeria was, thought Ghana was its capital city, thought "these new countries . . . creations of the British and French," and thought Nigeria "a large city" (America, 134-36).

On the other hand, knowledge of Africa seems to have irritated Clark almost as much as ignorance. An American professor of African literature stimulated Clark's special rage when he was unable to find on his own shelves the books that would resolve "some argument" about Nigerian authors. Clark "taunted him for trying to be smart with me." Later Clark learned the man was, at the time of the conversation, falling into total blindness. He seems to have been fairly well informed --but just not well enough.

Clark was, on another occasion, displeased with an Agency for International Development executive who knew Nigeria's political complexities well. The USAID man did not even subject Clark to a "torrential downpour of self-praise" that he implies he always got from Americans. The AID man's fault, it seems, was liking "being liked . . . by foreigners" (America, 139-41). Another American, recently returned from Nigeria, was objectionable because "he had himself all the answers" to questions about educational publishing in Clark's homeland. The quarrel--which kept Clark from eating his supper--is beyond reconstruction from Clark's comments on it, but it touched on Clark's opinions that the novel is not an African form and that English subject matter (English history, for example) should not be taught in schools. Again, the American was well informed--but not informed to Clark's taste.

Antagonistic as Clark is to Americans who make errors about Africa, he allows himself considerable freedom to be mistaken. He thinks the atom was split at "Alamo" instead of Los Alamos (America, 13); he thinks the 1913 construction of Princeton's Graduate College drove Woodrow Wilson to leave (America, 30), though Wilson was elected governor of New Jersey in 1910; he quotes "Frazier" instead of Thorstein Veblen for the phrase "conspicuous consumption" (America, 77); he calls AT&T "the American Telephone Company (America, 106); he says Albert Einstein was the first director of the "Institute of [sic] Advanced Study" (America, 112), but Einstein was only a member; he imagines a "weekly dole from the Social Security people" for an unemployed actress (America, 115); he thinks the nineteenth-century "robber barons" accumulated "billions" (pennies perhaps? America, 119); he implies that the AFL-CIO lacks black members (America, 180). These and other gaffes (like unintended inaccuracies in this study) might be passed over in silence if Clark himself was not so easily unsettled by American errors. One must suppose that Clark wrote America, Their America in the kind of passionate haste that scoffs at detail. Neither precision nor fine logic seems to have been important to his intention.

His disregard for logic is nicely illustrated in his criticism of programs that bring foreign students to American schools and universities. Particularly offensive to him was "a super drive" by "the American African [sic] Institute" to train promising African youth. Clark notes two major faults: first, the students should study at home, and, second, the students should be allowed to stay in the United States for postgraduate study. The program, Clark alleges, took students away from African universities in need of students and then denied these same students the qualifications for home government appointments. Another fault according to Clark is that not all the African students were placed in America's best universities. Finally he adds that the students learn what they do not need to know (America, 156-59). Some of these suggestions are so absurd as to render it doubtful that Clark intended them seriously. When later he urges that the American benefactors put their money into African institutions instead of paying the fees of African students, he seems quite serious, however, even though he provides no insight into the economics of

Clark's Parvin Year 67

educational transfer. Perhaps later, after himself becoming Professor of English, Clark would have criticized more modestly.

The immodesty of Clark's criticism, and its occasional absurdity, should not obscure the fact that he sometimes hits a real target. For example, he recognizes that the United States Supreme Court is an admirable example of judicial excellence. But, he rightly goes on, the bottom of the system can be "close" and "oppressive" upon the ordinary citizen, who lacks the resources to protect himself if abused (America, 170-71). Yet it must immediately be added that this, like virtually all of Clark's trenchant criticism, he learned (or could have learned) in seminars at Princeton University, from books freely available--even assigned reading--to him and other Parvin Fellows.

The remarkable characteristic of Clark's book is not its criticism of America, which is often inaccurate and, when accurate, never original. Nor is the book remarkable as a personal journal of an African experience of the United States. The journal itself is so closely limited to what the author found irritating that it seems continually trivial. What sets America, Their America apart is the observer himself.

Clark and America. In a curiously apologetic "Introduction" to his book, Clark caught an accurately disarming note.

> What follows . . . , the charitable might say, is not so much the story of my host and his incredibly sumptuous establishment but the jaundiced and unsavoury account of the responses and reactions of one difficult, hypercritical character and palate, who, presented with unusually rich grapes in a dish of silver and gold, took deprecatory bites, and churlishly spat everything out and in the face of all. Perhaps so.

Having gone so far, he makes a further admission:

> Now that I have got the whole fare out of my system, I feel so much better [sic] that I went through with the experience and the opportunity of that visit to America. (America, 12)

Clark was so shaken by his "eviction" (as he calls it)

from America, that he could not deal with the experience objectively until he had let, not "the fare," but the venom out of his system. With his rage eased he could, like a housewife after a good cry, get about his business. As will be seen, his business was to investigate the traditions of his own home.

Can it be said that the American experience turned Clark toward this new direction? Certainly there is negative evidence that it did. Clark did not return to journalism—except of course for the writing of America, Their America, which cannot have taken long. Also Clark resumed writing poetry and drama. Though this work does not lead in any obvious way toward the study of Ijo, it does suggest that Clark was actively rethinking his career. Even more negative than the foregoing is the idea that expulsion from Princeton inspired his return to academic life at Ibadan, in some sort of self-vindication. Finally, revulsion against the mechanistic quality of American life may have inspired a return to his roots, to the relative harmony of settled traditional life.

The best expression of this last is not the prose of America, Their America but its poetry, those surprising periodic effusions most of which found their way, with many of the earlier poems, into A Reed in the Tide. One of the poems (omitted from later collections) shows Clark's reaction to mechanical New York.

It is the first in the volume. It compares New York to a busy but meaningless termite colony. It begins, however,

> Steel, stone, glass boxes! Not one
> A carton
> To handle with care!

The city becomes a "nightmare / of ladders beams, bolts, fumes, refuse" and the streets are

> Sparkling conveyor belts, turning,
> Churning, carrying like rapids
> The boil and market of a continent
> Incontinent . . .

Then the central image emerges:

> So rears

Clark's Parvin Year 69

>   The anthill
>   Into the rainbow sky--

It is populated with "anonymous" and "overburdened" citizens, with guardian "soldiers,"

>   But here,
>   Where is the care,
>   the pool,
>   the queen?
>   (<u>America</u>, 19-20)

What seems to excite Clark's reaction is that no organic metaphor suits mechanical America. He draws upon his experience of the gargantuan tropical white ant mound precisely because it, unlike New York, cannot live without its soul, its source of being, its all-creative mother.

  Other poems, to be discussed later, reinforce this suggestion that Clark was homesick for a land and a past that was both fresh in his memory and easily idealized if one were away from the disenchanting circumstances of being a Lagos newspaperman. Nigeria favorably contrasted with the unlovely streets, machines, and subways of the America that simultaneously excited and repelled Clark.

  It is unlikely that any such experiences influenced his writing of <u>The Masquerade</u> in America, unless it be that the play's richer lyric quality than <u>Song of a Goat</u> was inspired by nostalgia. But something quite different surely did help create the form and content of <u>The Raft</u>. <u>The Raft</u> shows Clark partially liberated from the archaic stage conventions inhibiting construction of the earlier plays. Further, it shows a willingness to play with ideas.

  The politicization of Clark's art is shown in poems written after the American experience had run its course, poems that again go beyond the idea of Africa as victim: "Emergency Commission," "His Excellency the Masquerader," and "The Leader" (<u>Reed in the Tide</u>, 22, 23, 37). These are prepared for in effusions that are clearly inferior, like the following "epitaph" for Washington, D.C.:

>   A morgue,
>   a museum--

>   Whose keepers
>   play at kings.

In *America, Their America* this poem is merely clever; it is unfelt. But such a poem is liberating. Clark's irony is his most passionate expression, and before America he had never used it on objects that stirred his emotions. Irony is, after all, a cold form, not a passionate one. Clark had to learn how to join feeling with his natural manner; his dislike of America gave him his pretext.

America, Their America will be read in the future (if it is read at all) as an idiosyncratic, inaccurate, perverse, and entertaining self-portrait of the artist as pampered guest. But for the reader of Clark's poems and plays, it is wonderfully useful as a transitional work. Before it, Clark was a precocious youth, astonishingly skillful in the creation of telling poetic moments. After the book--and all its venom and invective--Clark dares to speak in his own voice as an artist. It is a new and challenging voice. The new works will not be so popular as the old. They are harsher, less romantic; colder and less engaging. Most of all they reveal the man behind the mask--as does *America, Their America*.

The Masquerade

The first of the two plays Clark completed in America is *The Masquerade*, a sequel to *Song of a Goat*. How soon the idea of a second play occurred to Clark is unclear. He seems to have had no idea of a sequel when he published *Song of a Goat*. That text clearly implies that Ebiere survived the action but miscarried Tonye's child (*Song*, 42). The situation underlying *The Masquerade* requires the reverse: Tufa is the surviving son of a mother who died in his birth. Otherwise, the cases are identical: Tufa is the son of his mother's husband's younger brother and was raised by an aunt (great aunt, presumably) after the suicide by hanging of his father and the death in the sea of his uncle (*Masquerade*, 56-57, 68). Even the town of Tufa's origin is identified as Deinogbo, the town of *Song of a Goat*--though the identification is only tentative (*Masquerade*, 44, 59). Unlike many sequels, *The*

Masquerade shows no falling off of quality; if anything it is superior to the original.

One critical difficulty that readers may have in appreciating The Masquerade is a natural tendency to focus attention on Tufa, whom Umuko specifically calls the "masquerader," rather than on the protagonist, Diribi. An outline of the action will show how the error arises.

At the start (Situation One), three fisherman "neighbors" comment on the disturbed time of excess tide and ominous moon. Into their sight come the newly engaged couple, Tufa and Titi. The former is "the young dashing stranger" and the latter is daughter of a foremost man of the creeks, Diribi. Their love scene, witnessed by the unseen neighbors, inspires the fishermen to join the festivities. At Diribi's compound (Situation Two), they interrupt talk between Tufa and Diribi, and, when angry words ensue, they allege doubts about Tufa's ancestry.

By midnight (Situation Three A), Diribi knows the story and seeks to persuade Titi to abandon the match. Failing, he departs in anger. Tufa enters to the insults of Titi's mother, Umuko, who outfaces the youth. Before a shrine (Situation Three B), Diribi demands to know his fault, and, in spite of restraining words from Umuko and other women of the house, he resolves on killing his daughter.

In the morning (Situation Four) Diribi has killed Titi and is said to be hunting Tufa. Tufa refuses to flee. When Diribi at last enters he ignores Tufa, who however attacks. As they are wrestling, Tufa is mortally wounded by an apparently accidental discharge of Diribi's gun. Tufa dies and Diribi, it is said by the Priests present, will be taken to Forcados.

That Tufa is the first seen of the two principal male roles, and that he dies in the end, both seem to mark him as the tragic figure. Yet the present writer, preparing a production for the first all-Nigeria Festival of the Arts (Kaduna 1972), found the play inevitably dominated by the commanding figure of Diribi. Tufa is the masquerader, but the whole action is the masquerade, a classic ritual of deception, discovery, suffering and death.

Diribi is the only great man of the play. His priestlike role before Orise, the Sky-God (Masquer-

ade, 74) identifies him as having a special role in
the community. His daughter is the talk of the Neighbors; indeed one attributes the fearsome tide and moon
to the anger of the gods at her departure (Masquerade, 53). His family--in contrast to Tufa's--is "the
most solid in all the Delta" (Masquerade, 72). He
himself is a good man, kind and indulgent to his
daughter--even, as William Connor has argued (with some
European prejudice against commonplace affection),
bordering on incestuous feelings (3). He is at the
same time sensitive to any challenge to his distinction
and prestige. Above all, he is the passionate protector of the family he heads.

Western readers of Clark's plays may easily underestimate the validity of Diribi's defense of his family.
As was suggested in the first chapter, and as Clark
himself shows in Song of a Goat, a family cursed by
the gods is the subject of terrible, even terrifying
penalties. Diribi's plea to Titi reveals the deep base
of his passion, the family, the "one stem" that supports the race itself:

>   But consider the taint,
> The bad sap that must flow out
> Of one bough into the other, no, pollute
> The one stem that really is standing
> To bear the graft, what will become
> Of us all?
>   (Masquerade, 69)

The Western reader may ask the basis of Diribi's fear;
is not the damage limited to Titi herself? On the
contrary, the "pollution" affects the collateral
family, Titi's brothers and sisters, their offspring--
indeed all of Diribi's descendants. In Titi's defection, Diribi sees--accurately, according to Delta
tradition--the wiping out of a great line. Titi, he
says,

>   now seeks
>   To dam my path, even as I answer
>   The unavoidable call to the sea.
>   (Masquerade, 74)

Immediately after these words he invokes the ancestors.
They live on only through his devotion. He asks them

to witness his innocence, to witness in effect the lack
of any cause why he should not, like them, enjoy the
devotion of the living that gives continuing life to
the dead. He sees his path to the ancestors' immortali-
ty blocked by the actions of his wayward daughter.

Diribi's concern for the gods is not isolated in the
play. The Neighbor fishermen find it possible that the
dangerous tide and ominous moon are expressions of
angry gods at Titi's "abandoning" her people. More
ominous still is their suggestion that Titi is herself
(like Orukorere in Song of a Goat) a "mermaid of a
girl" (Masquerade, 53). If she is indeed, unknown to
herself, a bride of the sea, two things are accounted
for: first her long refusal of marriage to the many
mortal suitors, and second her sudden acceptance of a
tainted stranger to whom a lasting marriage is impossible. The jealousy of the sea is dangerous, a counterpart to its love. Tufa too, the sole survivor of a
cursed breed, may, in dying, be victim of the god's
love. A priest thinks it may be so (Masquerade, 87),
and Tufa is beloved, in respective ways, by Titi and
Orukorere, both themselves beloved of the sea. In
short, underlying the whole play is the attentive
presence of deities who have long interested themselves
in both families, Tufa's and Diribi's, two families
that come to their tragic destiny in Clark's plays.

Thus The Masquerade shares with Song of a Goat
something of the Greek tragic pattern in which great
houses like those of Atreus and Laios work out their
histories, or like Yeats's history of Cuchulain (The
Green Helmet, On Baile's Strand, The Only Jealousy
of Emer). Clark's pattern is not imitative, however.
As has just been seen, the action depends on Ijo
belief, and is firmly rooted in the Delta. The time,
too, is recent, as is seen in Tufa's commerce that
takes him as far as Lokoja (at the Niger-Benue confluence) and Diribi's fate to be taken "to him at Forcados" (Masquerade, 57, 85) for execution:

> They say
> He has stitches so strong
> They still and staunch the worst breach
> In the dam.

The time and location are thus Clark's own, not a
legendary past or a romantic land. In producing the

play, the present writer took care that scenery, clothing, and style should all be contemporary without unnecessary theatrical stylization, and performances likewise should be consciously as natural as the convention of performance in English permitted. The result was a lively production, with drums and song, the whole being enthusiastically well received.

The play performs very well. Not the least of its virtues is Clark's vigorous yet dignified free verse. Its range is broad enough to encompass the song of the fishermen in Situation Two, the lover's verbal dance in Situation One, Diribi's plea to Titi and his subsequent anger in Situation Three, and in a final contrast Umuko's mad song in Situation Four. It also can sustain, without inappropriateness, a borrowing from Shakespeare's Antony and Cleopatra as a Neighbor describes the meeting of Titi and Tufa:

> You shoud have seen their first meeting. It was
> In the market place. Nine maids all aglow
> With cam fresh from stem formed her vanguard train.
> Another four of a bigger blossom,
> All of them wearing skirts trimmed with cowrie
> And coins, mounted props for a canopy
> Of pure scarlet and lace, and cool under it
> Walked Titi, in fact some said afloat, doing the last
> Of her pageants.
> (Masquerade, 57-58)

The song of the fisherman has a wholly different tone:

> Ogomugoro, Ogomugoro,
> Young woman, take a man!!!
> No, I won't: She ran.

This song invokes a call for another song that tells the tale of a folkloric masquerade in which a proud maiden, reluctant to marry (like Titi), falls in love with a monster (like Tufa?) disguised as a handsome stranger:

> The transformation
> Was into a python later shot down
> By one who had loved her all her virgin
> Life. Oh, toss up the song!
> A jolly old song, oh!
> (Masquerade, 61-62)

Clark's Parvin Year

The tale, brilliantly condensed into a premonition of the action to follow, is delivered brightly to the accompaniment of rhythmic drumming and the dance of laughing guests.

A contrasting lover's conversation also evokes an anticipation of danger. Titi tells of the fireflies:

> In
> The dew pods they touch up among
> A thousand, drooping wings of grass
> I see a simple watermaid, and a wicked
> Wicked traveller between her and home.
> (Masquerade, 54)

Diribi's plea to Titi is a different modulation, a tender family man's speech as he explains why he was so slow to examine Tufa's history and, as in the other examples, hints of a less (or more) than natural occurrence:

> We were right in the thick of your happy rites,
> And someone, if I remember well, yes, I think
> It was your Aunt Toro who then was saying
> We must find you a man quick . . .
> . . . when lo, like a couple joined
> Together out of this world, you walked in
> With the man. You were such a match.
> (Masquerade, 67)

His rage requires a wholly different tone as he compares Titi and Tufa to coupling curs:

> The bitch was not in her bed, do you
> Get that? She is even now not asleep
> In the bridal bed I myself built for her before
> That mongrel ran in, tongues down, to foul us all.
> (Masquerade, 75)

A final example of Clark's modulation of tone is Umuko's song to a cat she cradles as if a child; throughout, her imagery is natural, that of a delta wife and market woman:

> Out of eyes of fish at fall
> Of flood sown by bastard
> Babies in sand sprang this tree . . .
> Fresh fish at tuppence

>   Who'll buy fresh, oh
>   Fresh fish at just tuppence.
>   (<u>Masquerade</u>, 84)

    Throughout the play, as these examples imply, Clark avoids histrionic excess. Rather than creating for the actors the difficulties of the goat sacrifice in the earlier play, Clark allows the tragic situation to unfold.
    Clark's plays retain the earthiness of his society, maintaining a delicate balance in plays that deal substantially in sex, sexual passion, and death. The talk of sex is frank and clear but never obscene, just as death is present and inevitable yet not performed. Violence, too, is always near the surface, and suffering--or the threat of suffering--is a constant in these early plays.
    Successful as <u>The Masquerade</u> is as a play, few people are likely to see it performed. Most will judge it, then, as a play for reading. The passages already cited show that Clark's verse reads well, and the plot as outlined earlier is certainly sufficient to hold interest. The play has also for the reader an often exciting image of a complex Ij<u>o</u> society. Though written in America--or perhaps because it was composed in an alien environment--<u>The Masquerade</u> in little space shows variety and style in delta life: the hard labor of fishing, the rites of marriage (fulfilled or not), the taboos and gods that influence family life, the role of wives and women in (what is also shown) the compound of a great man. It reveals the reverence and duty of such men as the priests, as well as the comic irreverence of poorer townsmen in a great house. It shows too aberration in the society, especially romantic love and the potentially serious consequences of it.
    It is evident that Clark's motive in writing his first two plays was in great part to celebrate traditional life, its emotions, its dignity, its suffering. His use of operative, valid concerns in present-day delta life and his transformation of them into an English-language medium brought together Clark's image of Africa and a vast potential audience. Properly seen, or read, the plays can bridge the cultural gap that divides the worlds of the delta and the people beyond.

The Raft

The second play that Clark wrote in America, The Raft, is a radical change from its predecessors in several ways. The characters are laborers rather than people of significance to their communities. They are neither cursed nor responsible for their predicament. Although the characters are doomed, their passing lacks tragic significance. While the play has dramatic energy, it lacks a plot in the conventional sense. In the play four men are adrift on a raft. One is lost when the raft divides; another seeks safety from a passing ship and dies under its stern wheel. The remaining two drift out to sea. The play, in short, involves no celebration of traditional life but is instead pessimistic, unheroic, and negative.

The play's dramatic energy is to be found in its poetry, which both localizes and universalizes the predicament of the lumbermen. As in his earlier plays, but with simpler, firmer, more earthy diction, Clark in The Raft takes the audience or readers into the delta world and enables them to share the experience of life bound to the great river. At the same time, the terrible drift of an uncontrolled craft symbolizes the human situation in a world no longer bound by traditional laws and values. Thus the Niger becomes the world of modern civilization--European and African--in a time of disillusion and collapsing faith.

Although it is, as Theo Vincent has said in the best single study of the play, an intolerable limitation to read The Raft as a purely topical commentary on Nigeria or Africa in the early 1960s (4), it is hardly likely that Clark wrote the play without consciousness of circumstances at home. As a practicing journalist in Lagos, Clark had lived amidst the general dissatisfaction of Nigeria's intellectual community with post-independence politics. The corruption of limited self-rule during the 1950s, described well by Chinua Achebe in his novel No Longer at Ease, had rapidly become what Achebe's Odili in A Man of the People called a "fat-dripping, gummy, eat-and-let-eat regime." However vigorously Clark might defend Nigeria against her American detractors, he was more passionately disturbed by the active cooperation of his government in maintaining, for the benefit of the few in great power, many of the worst and most oppressive practices of colonial government, and in the creation of yet new forms of economic oppression. Nigerian political life was dominated by the feudal North, whose leaders had been most reluctant in the 1950s to encourage Nigerian independence, and all too soon they demonstrated conclusively that they had no faith in democratic processes.

The failure of democracy occurred in May 1962, not even twenty months after independence was proclaimed. The occasion was an emergency session of the Federal Parliament, which first declared "a state of emergency" to exist in the Western Region of Nigeria, then suspended the Western parliament, and appointed an Administrator, who promptly took into political detention leaders of the opposition. There was, of course, no "emergency." The majority in the Western parliament had rejected their premier and chosen to replace him. His supporters had rioted in the House to prevent a vote. That riot was the pretext for crushing the opposition.

Clark's interest in this is clear. He was a citizen of the West, the West being one of the three regions of Nigeria. (More that half the country was in the North; the Niger roughly divided the South into East and West.) The opposition was led by Chief Obafemi Awolowo, who articulated the radical attitudes of Nigerian intellectuals. The crushing of his party, as well as his detention--and later his arrest for treason, his trial, conviction, and imprisonment--convinced a great part of the educated elite that there was no hope that democratic action could be effective in changing public policy. Drift, not corrective action, seemed to be Nigeria's immediate destiny.

Clark makes but one allusion to the "emergency" in America, Their America. Visiting the Washington Post, Clark told the editor that his story on the emergency, published the previous day, was six months old. New material, "barely a couple of paragraphs" however, was "about the treason trials" (America, 49). The last was an allusion to Awolowo and other opposition leaders. Clark says nothing more of Nigerian affairs because his subject is America, but "the treason trials" are a reminder of the disintegration Nigeria was undergoing as the 1962-1963 academic year progressed at Princeton.

There is however no allegorical correlation between the characters in The Raft and personalities or entities in Nigeria. Clark himself has said that the political allegory, if it exists at all, was no part of his composition of the play, but "maybe subconsciously I was thinking about all this" (5). The play's pessimism, on the other hand, and the responses of the play's characters to their situation of danger and drift can easily be seen as colored, but not defined, by Clark's sense of the political dangers and the futility of domestic responses to it.

The corruption of Nigerian civil life is a major theme of the play. The four lumbermen are victims of their society, as R. N. Egudu has argued (6). At the same time, however, they are representative of the society, and Kengide, the dominant character who most forcefully decries the corruption, is himself thoroughly corrupt:

> In this game
> Of getting rich, it is eat me or I eat
> You, and no man wants to stew in the pot,
> Not if he can help it.
> (Raft, 120)

His corruption, like the Nigerian civil disorder of the 1960s, is defensive as well as offensive. Everyone is victim in a sum-zero political game.

The drama as a whole can best be understood through the characters. Kengide is, apparently, the oldest of the four. His cynicism seems based on his long life and experience. He sees through the self-deceptions of the others. When Olotu, the leader of the group, says he "hired" Kengide, the latter replies abusively

> Slime and entrails!
> And every fool that ever set foot on this raft
> Are on the same payroll, and the man
> With the purse is up wining away at Warri.
> (Raft, 96)

He is old enough to have participated in "the Great Strike" of the 1940s, through which he learned that government and business—"the Niger Company," Kengide's employer—were "two faces to one counterfeit coin," united in raising taxes and store prices while lowering prices on crops (Raft, 130-31). As if his work experience were not enough to make him cynical, his wife was both barren and promiscuous; "A reed in the tide," he calls her (invoking the title Clark would give his new collection of poems).

Oluto, "our captain" on the raft, is younger, better traveled, school educated, and more optimistic than Kengide. He is a "townsman" who has traveled among the great commercial cities of Lagos in the Southwest, Kano in the North, and Onitsha on the Niger (Raft, 111-12, 94, 96). In his sophistication he lacks Kengide's homely superstition. When the raft breaks up, with Olotu on the separated part, his loyalty to his job costs him his life: he cries out, "I can't leave the logs!" It is likely too that he cannot swim, and he cannot hear Ibobo's plea that he lower the sail.

Ogro is the most attractive character of the four. Called a "blundering bullock" by his comrades at the start, it is he who discovers that the raft is adrift (Raft, 91-92). He is the best sailor aboard (Raft, 121), and appears to be possessed by a god or ancestor (Raft, 105). He calls himself "Ogrope, born in the laps / Of the nine rivers and still suckling / On their breast" (Raft, 106). He upsets Olotu by offering his own excrement to use for bait (Raft, 107), but he is clearly right in seeing an effective if repellant means of dealing with their loss of provisions. Above all, Ogro is the singer, the deepest in his share of the traditions of the delta (indeed, he even sings one of Ozidi's songs, well before Clark had manifested an interest in pursuing that saga; Raft, 114).

The death of Ogro is the most pathetic incident of the drama. Ogro's infectious good humor and enthusiasm appeal to the audience more than to his comrades, but even they are moved to anguish when the stern wheel of the Niger Company boat captures his helpless body. Clark has created the pathos through Ogro's excited memory of children's games with the ships and sailors:

>   Oh it's fun to jump overboard
> And climb on again, out and in, out
> And in, to the loud cheers of the sailors till
> The last puff of smoke is out among the clouds
> Above the trees many bends away. Then
> And only then is it time to take the final plunge,
> Your arms full of gifts from the kind captain
> And his men.
>   (Raft, 117)

But Ogro is no child; he is a "full naked, brown bull," and the sailors beat his hands off the boat while Kengide and Ibobo watch in horror (Raft, 118).

Ibobo is the play's priest figure. While Ogro is full of delta lore, Ibobo is "the boy from the bush full of taboos," as Kengide says (this is in reference to Ibobo's incredulity about a description of male homosexuality; Raft, 127). Ibobo anticipates a successful landing at Burutu with a promise to sacrifice a goat to his grandfather.

But it is always Kengide who dominates. When Ibobo poetically observes the lights of Burutu,

> Oh the tall lamp-post you see in townships
> And the lovers in each others arms bathing
> In their glow,

Kengide replies,

> You should see crabs out of their holes
> In the peat and swamp, making splendid
> Salutations with hairy forearms under those
> Same lamps. And the scorpions never stop
> Stalking below the windows aglow with light.
>   (Raft, 124)

That reply shows accurately the quality of the mind that controls the others. For Kengide does control. It was he who refuses to allow Olotu to tie the raft securely, fearing "Visits from snakes and monkeys or worse" if the raft were made fast (Raft, 94). He rightly rejects Olotu's hope of escaping the Osikoboro whirlpool by punting (Raft, 101), and he plots their ebb-tide escape from the Ramos toward the Forcados River to Burutu. But when the wind and bamboo mats break up the raft, Kengide prevents Ogro from going to Olotu's rescue, warning of sharks in the water. He is less successful in controlling Ogro later, when Ogro makes his doomed swim for the Niger Company stern wheeler, but he does control Ibobo's final attempt to prevent disaster.

At the play's end, Ibobo and Kengide expect to land at Burutu, but are suddenly fog-bound. Ibobo chooses to jump and swim, but Kengide forcibly holds him. Ibobo fights fiercely, but Kengide's imagination is in command. He demands why Ibobo would "want to jump blindfold / Into a well full of snakes and stakes?" He accuses Ibobo of his own fear, for he himself is afraid "to be left alone / In this world." So they fruitlessly cry that they are "adrift and lost" as the raft proceeds out to sea.

It is not facile to see in Kengide an allegorical significance. His is the ignorant cynicism, corruption, and fear that was disrupting Nigerian life and displacing the hopes for independence in educated men, for whom Olotu may stand; the same hopes in traditional men of good will, like Ogro with his childish faith in the commercial ship's captain; and hopes in religious men like Ibobo. Clark was not a prophet. He certainly never saw Olotu's drifting away as an anticipation of the Biafran secession (to be discussed in the chapter on Casualties). Rather, The Raft is Shakespearean in conception, for in Shakespeare's plays character is both personal and symbolic.

The play succeeds because its allegory is never intrusive. As Clark has said, "I was trying to create a human condition which I knew existed not only in Nigeria but elsewhere" (7). Among the places it existed, of course, was America--where there has never been a shortage of Kengides manipulating and controlling her social and political life, and, through the power of the great bombs, the social and political life of all the world. As Kengide himself says, not perhaps knowing to whom he alludes, other than "white men":

> Now to prove their point
> They use something which my sister's son at college
> Says can turn the whole world into one pot
> Of mushroom soup--yes, even as you snap
> Your fingers
>
> (Raft, 127)

The Cuban missile crisis, as well as Nigerian conditions, helped to shape The Raft.

A Reed in the Tide

The first collection of poems in English by a West African poet to be published in book form by a major international publishing house was Clark's A Reed in the Tide, which appeared in 1965. At last poetry joined West African fiction and drama as a literary

form, written in the English language, that Africans--
or at least one African--could master. The volume
brought to international attention Clark's quality and
variety.

More than half the thirty-three poems had appeared
in the Mbari Poems, which was discussed in an earlier
chapter. Of the remainder, seven were part of America, Their America, and the remainder appear to have
been written during the Parvin year, or inspired by
events during that year--though only "Cave Call," a
poem about New York's subway trains, has an American
setting.

Overall, the poems are more political than those in
Poems. They are clearly a response to Clark's recent
engagement in Lagos journalism and to the disengagement
and distancing that followed. "Flight Across Africa,"
apparently on the first leg of his journey to New York,
sees "Earth . . . slaughtered" below; roads are scars
on the body, and the sacrificed land shows "valley and
/ Fields, . . . ulcerated in the sun."

Several poems are directly about events occurring in
1962. A commission of inquiry was set up after the
State of Emergency in the West had been declared (see
above). This is the "Emergency Commission" of Clark's
poem. Its report, issued late in 1962, showed "a
centre too rotten / For rings," as Clark puts it, and
"yet another tree that / Seemed beyond reach of wind /
And bolt, topples down." The "tree" may be an allusion
to Awolowo himself, whom the commission report implicated in improper use of government funds for political
party purposes.

Awolowo is certainly "The Leader" in the poem of
that name. In A Reed in the Tide, the poem is the
last of the volume; in A Decade of Tongues Clark relocated it to follow "Emergency Commission" and precede
"His Excellency the Masquerader," a poem about
Awolowo's rival of many years, Dr. Nnamdi Azikiwe. It
is useful to see the poems as a group. If Awolowo was
a tree in "Emergency Commission," he is something more,
yet fallen, in "The Leader."

> They have felled him to the ground
> Who unannounced home from abroad
> Wrestled to a standstill his champion
> Cousin the Killer of Cows.

The lines allude to Azikiwe, who, in his home area, would be greeted with the honorific Ogbuefi, or cow-killer (a reference to the feasting that accompanies certain ceremonies in Eastern Nigeria). Azikiwe was a famous journalist by the time he entered politics, after his education abroad. In contrast, Awolowo built his power base quietly before "he rallied the race and clan"--an allusion to Awolowo's strength among the Yoruba-speaking people.

> Now like an alligator he lies
> Trussed up in a house without eyes
> And ears

as a result of a trial (November 1962 to June 1963) which eventually convicted Awolowo of treason. He was not released until after the second military coup of 1966 (see chapter 5).

The sympathetic concern for Awolowo is contrasted with the extreme hostility toward Azikiwe, who was President of Nigeria. In "His Excellency the Masquerader," the fact that the Nigerian head of state (like the queen in England) has no real power is implied in the last stanza:

> The masks!
> O take off the mask! And behind?
> What wind! What straw!

Upon independence, Azikiwe had been something of a national hero, and his political party was in an alliance with the powerful party of the North. The alliance was shaken, however, after the State of Emergency in the West. When Awolowo had been controlled, the Northern Peoples' Congress had little further need for Azikiwe and his party. Ironically, the party had strongly supported the moves to control Awolowo. This helps to account for Clark's bitter language, including reference to a rusting bridge:

> And steel that should be blue
> At close grip
>
> Shows brown . . .

like the bridge across the Niger that linked Azikiwe's

Onitsha home with the Western Region. In this, as in other political poems, the imagery is vigorous enough that one is not compelled to seek out their referents in order to enjoy them.

An especially good example, a rather baroque poem (in Hopkins's manner) that the present writer likes but does not claim to understand, is "Who bade the Waves," in which Clark seems to speak in his proper person:

> No! my heart
> That is no stallion
> Or lion in its cage
> Encased with slab of stone,
> Rears in no rage
> But against itself that cannot
> Devour, savour all.

There is profound hopelessness, too, in what appears to be a reference to Christ:

> Who holds out hand
> Of deliverance, drank
> Dreg, paled upon nails, sank
> In dust. And the body
> Flames out still a thousand tongues, blind
> As waves, deaf as dunes. Oh why
> Does their cup fill out wind,
> And I
> All boiling with stone?

Certainly the tone invites comparison with the state of mind implied in <u>America, Their America</u>. If Clark began his journey in such a frame, America could never have pleased him. Though the tone is not pleasing, the poem succeeds because of the accuracy with which it describes and evokes real and passionate feeling.

The <u>America, Their America</u> poems are all, directly or indirectly, political and satiric. Not surprisingly, Cuba is recurrent and, with it, the "mushroom"--the atom bomb. The third "mood" of "Three moods of Princeton" (in <u>America, Their America</u> 34, in a slightly different form; not reprinted in <u>Decade of Tongues</u>) combines an appreciation of snow with dislike of the earth beneath it:

>   Snow,
>   Away
>   From my window
>   By time of waking,
>   What deft, gentle hands spread
>   You over this bed
>   Of bile, while we slept? And say,
>   Nurse, when shall the corpse lie?
>   There, ding, dong, ding--
>   When all the world is a mushroom pie.

Overall, the later poems in <u>A Reed in the Tide</u> are transitional. Clark had matured since <u>Poems</u>, and his artistic powers were growing, but the plays are far better representations of his maturity than the poetry or prose. The poems are, like the prose, responses to moments of disquiet. Their range is limited: they evoke rather than reveal.

Chapter Four
The Ozidi Complex

When Clark returned to Nigeria in 1963 he had, contrary to the Parvin director's expectation, no journalistic post to resume. His resignation from the Express group had, apparently, been final. His resumption of drama and poetry, however, and the experience in America, joined with Clark's old negritudist interest to lead him toward the study of Ijo tradition.

The first issue of African Notes (October 1963), a publication of the Institute for African Studies at the University of Ibadan, carried a brief notice titled "The Azudu Saga." It reports that Clark is a one-year research fellow at the Institute with a projected recording of "the traditional literature of the Ijaw people." Clark's own report follows:

> The Azudu story is one of Ijaws of the Western Niger Delta have heard told with great reverence and enjoyment among their nine clans for several generations. It is the story of a hero born to avenge the death of a famous father at the hands of treacherous rivals and friends ranging from men to monsters.

He goes on to identify "Azudu's grandmother Oreame" as the source of supernatural power in the story, and later he alludes to "Ozidi," a name by which Azudu "is sometimes called." Finally, Clark suggests "not just the tape recorder or bound volume" as the result of his project, "but perhaps a full-length color film" to "catch and convey something of the complete, complex and magnificent texture that is the Azudu epic."

Soon, Clark had three versions. And later he created a fourth--Ozidi, a play in English--then much later provided a fifth, his translation into English of the first version he collected. The play was the first published, in 1966. The translation appeared eleven years later, and at about the same time a film of an Ozidi festival performance that Clark and Frank Speed made in 1963 became available, as did a three-record

87

album of the music of the same performance. All of
these need to be taken into account in assaying Clark's
achievement.
   This chapter will first deal with Clark's translation of the Ozidi Saga, with reference where appropriate to the other versions, and then examine the play.
A third section will discuss the rhetorical derivation
of the play from the festival and saga, and the principles governing that derivation. The individual
elements of the Ozidi complex do not easily lend
themselves to independent discussion. As a result some
overlapping in the discussion cannot be avoided.
   Also, in shifting from text to text, spelling may
change. Throughout this chapter the spelling of any
name will be the spelling from the text identified at
that point. Usually the change is no more than the
use, or nonuse, of diacritical marks. Orea of Clark's
play, for example, is much the same person as Ore̱a
of the Saga; the marks discriminate the source. (The
relevance of diacritical marks to pronunciation is a
matter beyond the scope of this book.)

The Ozidi Saga

   The last version of Ozidi's story that Clark published is the second he heard, that of O̱kabou.
Before a detailed discussion of the Saga, a review of
Clark's first experience of the story will be useful.
   The Afoluwa Version. Clark first became aware of
the Ozidi tale when he was a schoolboy in the 1940s at
Ofonibe̱ngha. In the Preface to The Ozidi Saga,
Clark tells of seeking out Afoluwa almost twenty years
later, to hear again from him the tale he told the
schoolboy. This second performance was, however, disap-
pointing. Clark was fresh from hearing O̱kabou's
version and Afoluwa had long before become a seaman and
was so unaccustomed to the role of storyteller that his
Lagos neighbors were surprised at the occasion. The
result, Clark found, was that "he had forgotten the
script in its proper sequence of cause and effect"
(Saga, xv).
   Very likely Afoluwa's original version was less full
and logical than Clark recalled. As a schoolboy, he
was too young to have been critical, and the Ozidi tale
would have delighted a child's imagination even in
abbreviated and illogical form. Clark nowhere more

specifically describes the tale Afoluwa told, but it is reasonable to suppose that he had the main action well enough in mind. It would have gone much as the other versions do:

   The war hero Ozidi protests against his idiot brother's being named king of "Ado," but, when the thing is done, he demands that the new king be honored as tradition requires. For this insolence, the war chiefs of the town murder Ozidi, using magic to overcome the hero's invincibility. Simultaneous with Ozidi's death, his wife/widow is pregnant with a new Ozidi. She flees to her mother, Ore̲ame̲, a great witch. The grandmother, Ore̲ame̲, trains the child in the arts of death and revenge, and she procures for him charms for invincibility and a sword appropriate to such a hero. Young Ozidi returns to his father's town, avenges the murder on the many guilty warriors, and then fights other enemies until at last he confronts the terrible Smallpox King. Even Smallpox, however, falls Ozidi's victim at the end.

   That is the tale that caught young Clark's imagination. His own situation may have made the Ozidi story especially compelling to him. He had not long before been taken from the care of his own grandmother, his mother's mother, and brought to school. The loss of his grandmother would have excited in him a connection with Ozidi, also reared by a grandmother--a grandmother who magically raised a child to magnificent heroism and power. In such a way are the dreams of schoolboys made to seem real.

   Afoluwa told the tale as a story of Ado, the legendary imperial city known to history as Benin. This is in accord with the custom of itinerant storytellers who, according to V. C. O. Jituboh, traveled from town to town, with retinues of musicians, singers, and drummers, acting out tales of mythical Ado in a kind of monodramatic costumed spectacle (1). Ado, Clark says, is "the conventional setting of Ijo̲ tales and fables . . . the embodiment of all that is distant and mysterious, the empire of improbable happenings that together with the world of spirits help to explain the events of [the Ijo̲ peoples'] own lives" (Saga, xvii).

   Afoluwa may have heard other tales of Ado, but it seems likely he knew this one best and told it simply. He had no retinue. The choice of tale would be natural. To the Ijo̲, according to J. B. Egberike,

Ozidi is of special importance, "a household word with
definite archetypal associations which instinctively
spring to mind whenever the name is invoked as a title
or slogan" (2). (Indeed, at present there has been for
years a highly popular recording group in Nigeria
called "Ozziddi.") The tale, Egberike and Clark agree,
is said to have been communicated to the high priest of
Tarakiriye at Orua generations ago, perhaps as early as
the founding of the clan. The story told by Afoluwa
then is virtually eternal, originating in the beginning
of things as they can be recalled today. Such an
origin makes the tale a part of the sacred order of
things. Ozidi in a multitude of versions--a different
one for every teller, a variation for every occasion--
seems to be a, or the, central legend of the Ij̱o, "a
cultural myth of heroic conquest and territorial expansion," Egberike says.

If Egberike is correct in the words just quoted,
then it follows that the tendency among critics to call
Ozidi an example of oral epic poetry may be justified.
Most recently Isidore Okpewho has done so in his The
Epic in Africa. Discussing Clark's translation of the
Saga in the context of the classical European oral
epic, Okpewho finds marked parallels in the image of
the hero, the form and structure of the tale, and in
the particulars of the oral narration style. Further,
Afoluwa's version, though truncated and incoherent,
seems necessarily to have contained the elements that
John William Johnson has suggested may be essential to
the category. His paradigm requires that oral epic
poetry be (1) poetic, (2) narrative, (3) heroic, and
(4) legendary (there is a problem about this last, to
be returned to in a moment). Secondarily, it (5)
should be of substantial length, (6) serve a variety of
functions (social, sacred, entertaining, political,
etc.), (7) be transmitted within a culture as a rein-
forcement of the culture and its traditions, and (8)
employ a variety of literary forms or genres (narrative, song, proverbs, etc.) (3).

All recorded versions of the tale conform, unless it
be objected that Ozidi is not in fact an historical
person, is not "legendary." That the priest of
Tarakiriye received the tale in a trance or dream seems
to deny Ozidi historical significance. Yet curiously
the names in the Saga are Bini names, from Benin,
with the significant exception of Odugu, who seems to

be Igbo. Ado, or Benin, is north of the Western Ijo place of origin for the saga. The Igbo live yet beyond the Bini-speaking people, north and east. This objective evidence of names requires a precedent legend. This together with the confidence of Ijo people in the validity (if not the objective truth) of the tale justifies Ozidi's being called "legendary" as well as "hero."

It ought to be objected that there is little use in applying European terms (like "epic" or "legend") to African cultural artifacts; such objection is fully justified. Unfortunately, failure to address the question may represent as great an ethic bias as raising it does. The important consideration is, in Hamlet's phrase, to discuss the matter "with modesty enough," never distorting the African form in an effort to make it meet unsuitable criteria, and using the European terminology only *faute de mieux*, as a means to understanding across cultural and linguistic barriers.

Accepting the word "epic," then, it is possible to see that when, in 1962 and 1963, Clark sought to recapture the experience Afoluwa first offered him so many years before, he was attempting to recapture something momentous at the heart of Ijo culture. Afoluwa could not give that experience to Clark a second time, but the situation was far from desperate. Clark had already in hand the version by Okabou Ojobolo.

The Okabou Version. It is not clear how Afoluwa learned the Ozidi story, but Clark has said that Okabou "carried the kit for Atazi" (Saga, xxxv) though he was never himself a bard by vocation. It is evident that Okabou was nevertheless accomplished in the art, and was prepared to tell yet other great stories, if Clark wished him to do so (Saga, 364, 390, n. 35). He was at the same time already over seventy years old, a frail link to the past (Saga, 156, n. 49), which he seems vividly to remember. In the narrative, Okabou credits two previous bards by name. One, intermediate or successor to Atazi, was "Ozobo." The seeming originator ("in its present form," according to Clark's note) was "Atazi who holds the front as the foremost bard" (Saga, 157, 156). Indeed Atazi's Story seems almost an alternative title: when Okabou is winding up his final night's narration, he attests how he was called to recite, yet he does not mention the hero's name: Madame Yabuku, he says, sent for him. She said, "Atazi used to tell a story, now Atazi is dead. / If you know it . . . come and tell it." He then adds, "Accordingly, I came, and I've told the story, right up to where I knew Atazi told it. / If I add some more, then I shall have told a false story" (Saga, 388). Thus Okabou certifies that he has told the true tale, "true" in the sense that it is as he himself heard it.

This cannot mean of course that a performance in Madame Yabuku's "sitting room at Inalende in Ibadan" was the same as the full show that Atazi and his retinue provided in their time. Okabou seems to have had minimal instrumental support; a drum or two seems all. His main support, apparently, was the women spectators functioning like a chorus (see Saga, particularly 270-73) with men joining in certain songs (e.g., Saga, 261, where the two groups seem distinct). Men functioned too as commentators, though the strongest voice in the audience seems to have been Madame Yabuku's. These "support" factors emphasize the improvisational character of the performance and show the impossibility of Okabou's in any sense duplicating Atazi's version. Further, age and perhaps relative inexperience result in a confused narrative at times (Saga, 38-39 is a good example). Clark in the introductory essay has noted "faults in repetition, faults of prolixity, faults from lapse of memory, faults crying aloud in the frequent paratactic constructions . . ." (Saga, xv) that mar the performance and guarantee that it, in the highest oral tradition, is unique.

The true story is what Okabou has preserved from Atazi; not more and not less. Clark finds in this version qualities absent from Afoluwa's tale as well as from Erivini's festival drama, recorded in the film Tides of the Delta, which will be discussed later. Okabou's version is complete and unified, Clark says, following (Aristotelian) rules that incidents must follow in proper relationship one to another. Further, there is "natural law and logic" in the crimes that Ozidi commits against himself, killing his uncle and, almost, doing as much for his mentor grandmother Oreame. This Clark finds more satisfying than the other versions that spare "Ozidi and his family and . . . leave Oreame undefeated in the field" (Saga, xv-xvii). There is a difference too in the location of the action. Instead of Ado, under the

The Ozidi Complex

insistent prodding of Madame Yabuku, Okabou locates his action at Orua. Yet even her watchfulness is insufficient: though she corrects him often, he nevertheless often slips, uncorrected, into calling the place Ado. Ado seems clearly where Atazi set the story--inappropriate water imagery and all.

The water imagery shows that the Saga is an indigenous Ijo work though set in Ado. In the canon of Clark's work The Ozidi Saga is unique in that it is so purely indigenous: Clark has labored to re-create, so far as the English language permits, the actuality of the Ijo text in his translation. There is no verbal tirckery, no oblique or cryptic allusion, no use of surprising rhythm, no flamboyant imagery. Even Clark's characteristic wit and irony are reserved for the preface, introductory essay, and notes. The reader of the English text senses that he is as near the actual circumstances of performance as the printed word is likely to bring him. A combination of the text, the Ozidi recording, and the film image creates a very rich feast indeed, to which the 1966 play is an aperitif.

The volume containing Okabou Ojobolo's version of Ozidi has three parts, preface and introductory essay, the Ozidi Saga in Ijo and English, and two appendices containing songs from other versions and the text of the film narration.

The essay may be dealt with briefly. Clark discusses technical problems of transcription. They are highly significant to the specialists in linguistics and, although they cannot be discussed here, controversial. He then deals with four areas of interest to the more general reader: the variant modes of presentation; the language and poetry; the music, mime, and dance in performance; and the festive and religious aspects of Ozidi. These four brief essays are apt to confuse the reader whose only knowledge of the saga is the text in this volume. Clark first observes that Ozidi may be performed as a bard's solo narrative or, equally, as a drama in which the narrator becomes the protagonist in a group of performers. Then, as he discusses characteristics of the Saga, he mingles rather indifferently the two modes. It often appears that Clark is describing the Okabou version when instead he is talking about the performance that was filmed. Some of the remarks, naturally, apply equally well to both, as when he discusses "the world view of the Ijo" (Saga, xiii-xiv). But the "masks and costumes" discussed (Saga, xiv) have nothing to do with Okabou's performing in Madame Yabuku's sitting room at Ibadan. The essay is nevertheless helpful in providing a context for the narrative.

The Saga itself is told in seven "nights," each representing several hours of performance by Okabou, interspersed with songs, chants, comments, and responses. The narrative is by no means simple and straightforward. It is a highly personal performance. The brilliance of Clark's translation lies to a great degree in the preservation of the liveliness and spontaneity of interaction among the crowd, tape recorder, drummer, researchers, and Okabou himself.

One example from Night Two well illustrates the freshness. It represents a moment in Ozidi's protracted fight with Azeza, the second of the murderers that Ozidi kills. It begins with Ozidi's declaration of intent, in which a single Ijo sentence--"Dau sowei ke emo biyime!"--is repeated five times. Clark provides four apparently appropriate translations (see note 30, Saga, 98). When the hero's uncle flees, Okabou calls upon the spectators to "sing into" the tape recorder (Saga, n. 31). The rest of the passage is clear enough. This is the whole:

> "Listen, I am Ozidi! I am Ozidi! Vengeance for my father is all I seek!
> Restitution for my father is all I am after!
> Rest is all I seek for my father. Justice for my father is all I ask."

Now, with all this happening, his father's brother, the moment he heard this, straightaway, Temugedege fled.

(Laughter)

Caller: O Story!

Group: Yes

With Temugedege fled like that, at his flight, shall we sing into it--
    Temugedege's song--and let the master-drum speak:

The Ozidi Complex

Song

Solo: Temugedege is coming!
Chorus: O shame, Temugedege!
(Repeated seventeen times)
Caller: O STORY!
Group: YES!

Temugedege on hearing the noise of the whirling sword [cried]:

"This man, this boy will cut me dead today."

(Laughter)

As he fled, [Ozidi] sped through the courtyard, with one flourish his sword clipped all the grass.
(Saga, 84)

The reader is given ample imaginative scope here. Okabou's vigor at the start, his miming of Temugedege's cowardice, the spectator's delight and encouragement, the conscious directing of attention to the tape recorder--then entry of the masterdrum and the mocking, antiphonal song (in Ijo, "Temugedege boyemee! . . . Oyaa Temugedege!")--next Temugedege's quavering fear again provoking laughter, and, finally, Okabou describing and miming Ozidi's hyperbolic sword stroke: all this is compacted into less than a page of text.

This liveliness has customarily been edited out of transcriptions of oral recitations, from classic Greek times to the present (4). Clark's daring originality in transcribing and then publishing everything recorded on the tapes is greatly to be admired. It arises perhaps from the fact that Clark is simultaneously an African and a rebel. Often it seems that European investigators are at pains to legitimize their transcriptions by sanitizing them, lest they lose dignity. An African might understand the epic form's informality yet be inhibited from revealing it. Clark has little inclination to be bound by precedent; he is as apt to break a mold as use it. He is faithful to the tape recorder, not convention. The result is extraordinarily interesting and at the same time demanding. It is a work of literature for study more than it is, as printed, entertaining.

Also, translation itself is a problem. Ijo does not readily translate into English, and the English equivalents of Ijo phrases are devoid of their Niger delta cultural content. Familiar English words conjure up English, not Ijo, ghosts, spirits, people, and things. In the opening lines of the saga, for example, Ozidi is called Orua's hero. It is said that he has "palemootu." In one line "palemootu" are "lieutenants"; in the next, "deputies." Obviously they are neither, in any English sense. And there is no way to exorcise the English connotations of the words.

So, too, with "pere," or "king" in Clark's translation. The action begins with the elevation of Temugedege to "pere," and the initial crisis is precipitated when Orua utterly fails to pay any attention to the "pere" at all. He is, again obviously, no "king" in any English sense, and it is impossible to guess from the text what sort of office "pere" might in fact be--other than that (1) it is for life, (2) it rotates among the seven districts of Orua (for which, read "Ado"), and (3) the holder of the title is customarily presented with the head of a male victim as a sign of his office, a prelude to the pere's being given money and a feast. Perhaps the office involves duties, since Ozidi attempts to refuse it for himself and his brother, but one would have to look elsewhere to discover what the duties might be (5).

The problem of pere is but a hint of the cultural obscurities the reader unconversant with delta lore must deal with, unaided by an explanatory apparatus that could well have doubled the size of the volume. Yet reading The Ozidi Saga in English alone is a rewarding experience.

It is most rewarding if, in reading the English, one keeps an eye on the parallel Ijo text. This is most obvious in the onomatopoetic passages. For example, after Ozidi has sliced up Azeza's wife, he sends her home with a message. The English text reads, "Oh, Azeza's wife rushed out there, all pieces cutting through the air," while the Ijo text reads more vividly, "O, Azeza ta wan duo para para para para para para pa pa pa pa pa vou vou vou vou vou" (Saga, 55). Again, recurring throughout the narrative is Ozidi's activation of the powerful charm of Bouakarakarabiri: "It boiled over with its cauldrons, now the hornbill scream, then the kingfisher notes, O Ozidi the grove! and now the boom of the monkey." This pales beside, "Pa gbe gidi gidi gidi dari go, godo godo godo godo

godo, kpeyaiin kpeyaiin kpeyaiin, dro, dro, dro, Ozidi woo bou! Kpingi Kpin" (Saga, 72).

Other original felicities appear untranslatable even though the verbal content can be rendered. The song that Tebesonoma's sister sings as she contemplates her imminent murder, is an excellent illustration.

Tamarau laa fe ke bo
    e ba de yo
	Death that has nothing
	    to do with God
	    is what is killing me

Tamarau laa fe ke bo
    e ba de yo
	Death that has nothing
	    to do with God
	    is what is killing me

Tebesonoma o ene
    kpekpe kene tobou
	All because of Tebesonoma,
	    my one and only child!
	    (Saga, 258)

It is unnecessary to hear the music in order to sense the musical tone of the song, which is lost in the literal translation. One suspects too that the ambiguity of the last line is an artifact of transcription or translation: Okabou would have shown in his pantomime that the "child" is in the singer's arms; it is not her brother Tebesonoma.

On the other hand, it would not be correct to say that Clark's verbal powers have been so constricted by his determination to translate literally that the Saga loses excitement. There is an abundance of incident that keeps the narrative at a high level of energy throughout.

It would not be practical to review the abundant incidents of the Saga's seven nights in detail. The story pattern is overall the same as the other versions. Since most readers of this chapter will be acquainted with the play only, what follows shows the content of each "night" and calls attention only to incidents that either are of special interest to readers of the play or otherwise make an instructive contrast to the play.

The action of the first act of Clark's play (and of nearly three days of the filmed festive drama) is covered swiftly by Okabou : on page 12, Oreame herself flies on her magic fan to tell Orea that she is pregnant, to bury the head of Orea's husband, and to carry Orea away. Ozidi is born on line two of page 13.

The remaining forty-five pages of Night One correspond to Act Two and half of Act Three of the play, with many of the same incidents (see below): target shooting, a leopard, a hill, the iroko tree, Bou-Karakarabiri, the discovery of Ozidi's name, the return to Orua, the blacksmith with the making of the sword (after the arrival at Orua rather than before as in the play; the play's order is the more logical), the incident with the wives on the road, and finally Ewiri's warning to the murderers that "A man wronged will often bear a strong son" (Ozidi, 57). In short, almost half of Clark's play parallels Night One alone.

Night Two tells of Ozidi's fight with Azezabife, like Scenes Five and Six of Clark's Act Three, but it also includes a preceding contest with Agbogidi as well as elaborate development of the circumstances around each fight. Okabou's art is particularly well shown in Night Two, as he narrates, acts, makes sounds of trumpets and charms, intersperses his narrative with songs, with aphoristic utterances ("O life, does God [Tamarau] create to kill?" Saga, 65), with boasts, and with commentary. The fight with Azezabife is greatly extended, and Oreame plays a much more effective role in it than Clark gives her in the play. Indeed, she does not merely pray to God for assistance, she "scaled the skies" and asked God--"Tamara"--directly what She thought of Ozidi's fight. And God answers personally and directly, telling her to go ahead with the fight (Saga, 82-83).

The end of the fight contains a suggestion of a fossil episode that Okabou does not develop. As this climax to the Night is a good example of the complexity that the narrative sometimes is burdened with, it can be described rather fully here. Azezabife has his one leg cut off, and then his head, and then is cut in two, but he recovers from these blows, just as Ozidi has recovered from having his own head cut off a moment before. At this point Oreame does a most peculiar thing. She flies home to Orea and strikes her daughter's belly with her fan. Orea becomes instantly pregnant, lies down, and delivers a baby. Orea goes indoors, leaving the baby on the ground. The next line reads, "Bringing out one unglazed pot, and shoving into it a new chicken, off she [Oreame] flew, with a glide." She lands on the field of battle and tells Azezabife, "'I am cutting you down right now.' / The moment she said she was going to cut him down, suddenly, the dazzle." This, "dazzle," apparently, renders Azezabife unable to move; Ozidi's slaughter song, in an esoteric language, follows; and Ozidi hurls away Azeabife's head (Saga, 95-97).

The fossil episode of the baby has an antecedent, in that for Azeabife certain things are taboo: "a chicken, a new-born babe, a pot not yet through the kiln . . ." (Saga, 78), but such a taboo implies a story of some sort that is not told by Okabou. The "dazzle" (his look at the objects) that controls Azezabife was (evidently) conveyed by Okabou with some powerful action. It evoked a response from the audience and led directly into the slaughter song. The complex interaction of story, action, response, and song creates the climax to Night Two, and leaves in it a good deal of mystery as well. Ozidi is a fabulous tale, as well as a heroic one (6).

In Night Three, Ogueren is Ozidi's first victim. He is Oguaran in the play, "possessed of twenty toes, / Twenty fingers" (Ozidi, 8). The fight is long and eventful. Badoba (whose song Okabou admits he has forgotten, Saga, 150) faces Ozidi after Akprobisi (the play's Agobogidi) has been disposed of. Okabou tires after two fights, so he eliminates Badoba in summary fashion.

Ofe is disposed of in Night Four, completing the action corresponding to Act Three of the play.

But the encounter between Ozidi and Ofe is wonderfully retarded by intervening conflicts. First, Ebeya (who does not appear in the play) proves to be almost powerful enough to kill Ozidi. Oreame had failed to anticipate him and Ozidi is helpless without her charms to protect him. Then Ozidi begins the fight with Ofe and has the momentary ill-fortune to be cut in two. He is quickly saved by Oreame's fan. The fight is suspended while Oreame and Ozidi find occasion to go for a stroll. He wears a beautiful wrapper and, anachronistically, a polo shirt (Saga, 181). Oreame for the occasion looks like a young woman. They are admired by Sigirisi (also called Fingrifin) but Oreame insults him. He takes the two captive. Oreame excites Ozidi's mortar-and-pestle charm, and the hero chops up his captor's altars and children before doing in the creature himself. Sigirisi lacks the net he uses in the play.

Killing Ofe proves quite difficult. In the play
Clark places the end of the fight on the fourth day.
In Night Four the fight progresses much more slowly,
and is interrupted for a seven-day week while
Oreame investigates among oracles for the secret
of Ofe's changing himself into a new thing every
time he is wounded. The seventh oracle tells her how
to break Ofe's protection. As in the play,
Oreame produces the needed fetish--but there is
no intervention as in the play by Tamara; Oreame
is just "fed up" (Saga, 200). Ofe is killed
immediately, and Ozidi terrifies the townspeople (killing a few) and they desert "Ado" (which a spectator
reminds Okabou should be called "Orua," Saga, 201).
Something of the same sort concludes the third act of
the play.

Since Act Five corresponds to the last fourteen
pages of Night Seven, it is evident that Clark com-
pressed Nights Five, Six, and most of Seven into his
Act Four. His handling of the first major episode of
Night Five shows remarkable compression. Ozidi's conflict with the Scrotum King is reduced to forty-odd
lines of reported dream. In the Saga, it is an hilarious account, spaciously developed. Ozidi and the
Scrotum King ineptly fight to a stand off.
Oreame, her wings making a "noise as loud as that
of an aeroplane" (Saga, 222), comes to the rescue.
She is, however, unable to help until an oracle gives
her the necessary charm. Then Ozidi kills the king,
producing a lake, as in Clark's Ozidi dream.

An important difference between the play and the
Saga is better revealed in this episode than elsewhere. It is that Ozidi does not age consecutively in
Okabou's version as he does in Clark's. Throughout
the Saga Ozidi is a "boy" who "plays," not the formi-
dable hero one expects. Ozidi becomes the hero only in
order to do battle under the influence of Bou-
Karakarabiri's charm, as the following extract shows:

> And his bowels again rose in rage [with the usual
>   onomatopoeia]
> And again the sword had since issued forth.
> Numerous were the magic belts bursting with power.
> If you saw the previously slender youth, he was now
> a sturdy and huge man. He had grown quite into
> man.
>   (Saga, 222)

In his ordinary self, he is a mere stripling, "a little twirp of a boy," as Odugu's wife says (Saga, 235).
   Clark in the play shifted the story of Odogu and his wife to the end of Act Four. In the Saga it begins after the Scrotum King episode and is interrupted by the meeting with Tebesonoma. Threatened by the seven-headed monster, Ozidi is a craven little coward, weeping and crying out for Oreame. As usual, she arrives in time to save him, and to hear Tebesonoma ask Ozidi to kill his sister. Leaving Tebesonoma alive, they proceed to the house of the beautiful young woman for the Saga's only scene of pathos.
   It parallels Clark's dramatic version. Ozidi is reluctant to kill the hospitable and innocent mother and child. Oreame incites him and he responds to the bowels charm, but the innocence of the woman again controls him. Not even Ozidi's horn blower can bring himself to encourage the hero. Oreame gives him yet another charm, the woman sings her death song (quoted above) and Ozidi slices mother and child with a single blow.
   Grandmother and grandson then return to a now-conciliatory Tebesonoma. He is forced to flee, but Ozidi pursues and cuts off his heads. Oreame, as in the play, scatters corn to bring the seventh head, a cockerel, into Ozidi's range. With that Night Five ends, leaving the episode of Odogu's wife in progress.
   Ozidi had been sexually excited by the woman; it was his first such experience. In the calm beginning of Night Six he goes out to "play"--being warned not to go toward Odogu's compound. Naturally, the callow youth disobeys and soon Odogu finds Ozidi "ensconced on the lap of his wife" (Saga, 277). Oreame learns of Ozidi's danger from an oracle she is consulting on behalf of a client (the fact that she is practicing divination and witchcraft for others is not noticed in the play, but is frequently alluded to in the Saga), and she flies into the compound and swoops out Ozidi, taking along the woman as well. This sets up the scene which Clark has written in the play as the fourth scene of Act Four: the woman's use of sex to entice Ozidi into revealing the source of his power. In the play Ozidi kills her fairly quickly. Okabou modulates Ozidi's behavior by having him on three successive

nights prepare to kill her but actually do so only on
the last. Each night he goes to his shrine, gets his
sword, and invokes his slaughter song--this last sung
sotto voce. The effect is delightful, an engaging
variation of the killing pattern.

The murder sets up the battle with Odogu, in which
the mothers (or grandmothers) of the warriors directly
compete, since the warriors are equally protected
against each other. Ozidi uses the wife's corpse to
taunt Odogu with until the latter's "mother" carries it
off and buries it. Odogu weeps because he is too ugly
to get another wife (Saga, 302). When the two fight-
ers are utterly exhausted, Oreame (using better
wings that the opposition witch) gets the herb necessary to revive Ozidi (Clark in the play has Bouakaraka-
rabira tell the women about it). The result is that
Ozidi kills them all, including Oreame. At that
point, Clark's Act Four ends. Night SIx of the Saga,
however, sees Ozidi regret Oreame's death and his
blind rage. And, in contrast to the play, Oreame
saves herself by advising him in a dream how to bring
her back to life.

Night Six also introduces Tebekawene, Ozidi's
next opponent and (like several predecessors) a canni-
bal. This monster is evidently the original of Clark's
stage direction description of Bouakarakarabiri in the
play (Act Two, Scene Five): "He is a half-human character who can walk on his head." This matches
Okabou's "He stumped upon his head, his feet swing-
ing in the air." Both have pots boiling in expectation of cooking Ozidi (the play, 42; Saga, 328-31).
Ozidi's reaction to the creature in the play is scorn-
ful, obscene, and insulting. In the Saga, the boy
Ozidi is, as usual, terrified, though in both versions he calls attention to the odd position of the
monster's anus (Ozidi, 42; Saga, 334). The meeting
of Tebekawene and Ozidi occurs near the start
of the seventh and final night. Ozidi is helpless in
the play and Saga until Oreame intervenes by
rooting the monster's feet to the ground. The correspondence goes no further. Tebekawene is so
quickly dispatched that Okabou is faced with a near
revolt as no fewer than six separate spectators enter a
debate as to the adequacy of the report (Saga, 338-
39). It is a remarkable example of the spontaneity
that marks the narrative as a whole. It marks also the

The Ozidi Complex

fact that the inventiveness of the old man had eventually begun to ebb (he wishes the tape would run out "before I lose myself," Saga, 342).

He perseveres, however, going on to the tale of Azemaroti. This adventure pits Oreame, disguised as a young and beautiful girl, and her apparent beau Ozidi against an incestuous mother-son pair of cannibals. The son predictably lusts for Oreame but the mother is adamant that the whole Ozidi party (hornblower and drummer included) must be cooked. From this episode, no doubt, a psychosexual hypothesis regarding the African mind will eventually evolve; the present writer can only pray that any such "Ozidi complex" will be received with extreme skepticism. It is not in reference to this episode that the present chapter has been named. The episode is an extended one, with Okabou at his best in providing fresh battle material. It ends with nearly a third of Night Seven remaining.

The ending centers around the slaying of the Smallpox King. This episode, and its divergence from other versions, can better be dealt with later. This is the place, however, to note the curious interjection at this late point of a wife for Ozidi. The wife episode seems more than an expansion of the tale to fill the night's narrative yet less than an integral part of the Ozidi hero tale.

Oreame brings the girl forth by magic, and the bride herself seems more than merely natural. Oreame "struck the ground with her fan, and a girl came walking in, like a goddess out of the stream" (Saga, 371). A water spirit as a wife for Ozidi would seem wholly appropriate, but the plain fact is that nothing is made of the magical origin, and Okabou quickly drops her as a subject in order to tell, in comic fashion, how Ozidi, shamelessly and without retribution, murders his helpless (but annoying) uncle Temugedege. Then Ozidi is said to laze around with his wife (Saga, 375) until the Smallpox King becomes interested. Instantly the wife vanishes: the King will visit Ozidi who "lives . . . alone with his mother" (Saga, 376). The wife reappears as Ozidi' s companion at the arrival of Smallpox (Saga, 377), and, when Ozidi is struck down by the disease, his wife urges him to get up and does not know what to do (Saga, 378, 379). Orea then recalls that Ozidi has

not had yaws, and Oreame finds the cure. Ozidi's
wife expresses pleasure that Ozidi is getting up (Saga, 384). When Ozidi has slaughtered the whole smallpox crew and exulted at length, he (in a one-line final reference) embraces his wife (Saga, 387). Though not forgotten by Okabou, the wife is utterly nonfunctional. Clark wisely omitted her from his play.

That Ozidi should have a water spirit bride, however, is an interesting variation for the tale. It is a reminder that Ozidi is an Ijo folk hero whose legend extends far beyond the stories Clark has, in one way or another, reproduced. Whether there is, in fact, somewhere an episode of Ozidi's marriage, with the probable complications attendant on marriage to a mermaid, or Okabou recalled another hero tale entirely, is uncertain. The narrative is alive and changing: perhaps the story of Ozidi's marriage has yet to be told.

Ozidi the Play

Reading Ozidi effectively requires a strong aural and visual imagination. The demands upon the reader are of a different kind than the demands of Clark's earlier plays. The earlier plays had few stage directions; as a result, movement had to be inferred from the spoken lines. Though ingenuity was necessary, the action itself was clear. Music and dance were minimal. In contrast, the stage directions in Ozidi, the properties, movement, music, and dance, are extraordinarily detailed. Indeed, the play is quite as much to be visualized and heard as it is to be read.

For the alien reader, the demands upon aural and visual imagination cannot easily be satisfied. The English words Clark uses to describe what is to be heard and seen cannot evoke the images Clark knows from experience, without some assistance beyond the play text. Fortunately visualization and hearing can be helped by means of the film Tides of the Delta, subtitled The Saga of Ozidi (As Recreated by the Ijo People of Toro-Orua and Bulou-Orua in the Bendel State of Nigeria, and Recorded by J. P. Clark and Frank Speed), the "Commentary" to which is printed as an appendix to The Ozidi Saga (Saga, 401-8). It opens with several minutes of introduction to the people of the river and their environment. Then the Ozidi performance begins. As in Clark's play, the action starts with a ritual procession to the river with gifts for the water spirits. Throughout the film, the spectator sees the narrator and protagonist (as in the play) speaking, moving, and acting, often to the accompaniment of music, song, and chant. He wears--in the language of the play's opening stage direction--"<u>a white flowing shirt and tunic</u>," and he is assisted in the performance by a great variety of men and women, often spectacularly costumed, who in dance and pantomime augment the narrator's performance. An audience is always present in the film, as the play too requires, and the setting in the play and film is like that described by Clark in his introduction to the Saga: the stage is

> the open public square of the market place, uncluttered by scenery and free for the great imaginative act to come to life. The story-teller-protagonist has only to wave his fan before the audience, point his sword across the river, and the ancient city-state of Orua rears to life with broad highways spanning the wide expanse of swamps and stream. In the same spirit of evocation, violence, so dominant in the saga and providing a constant source of threat to players and spectators alike, is either reported or represented in dance and mime.
> (Saga, xxiv)

The dance and mime, like the setting itself, cannot be found on the printed page or in the uninitiated imagination. The film is not essential to reading or even understanding the play, but it makes possible a fuller experience, closer to the Ijo original. Erivini, the actor-narrator of the film, evokes the practical world of performance which Clark's stage directions, as will be seen, often evade.

The First Act. The principal function of the first act is less to tell the Ozidi story than to bridge the cultural gap between Orua, the Niger delta locale of the play action, and the reader. The narrator's opening monologue is effective in starting the process. The sacrifice to the gods must be carried by seven virgins, the narrator says, and then immediately he adds an acknowledgment that many spectators will find such an action "a quaint custom," a "propping up" of "cobwebs that with broom and brush we ought to sweep clean out of the house." The objection noted, he declares that piety will not permit deviation from custom, and the ceremony proceeds. Clark's easy lines allow the narrator self-deprecation, admiration for the virgins, and some boasts for his people. The lines as well have considerable charm through which the reader is effectively drawn into acceptance of the play's conventions.

This acceptance is reinforced after the ceremony by an old woman who, with a broom, seeks to sweep away malign influences (spirits, but perhaps people as well) whom no sacrifice will sweeten: "Let them go off at once / In great speed, yes, in great speed / For we do not seek to please them." When she has repeated her spell, the drama proper begins. While she was speaking, palm wine was being distributed among the dancers and actors, including the storyteller, and when she is finished, the group take on character and become the Orua Council of State, in heated discussion of the pressing need for a king. The transition is complete.

The problem the Council has is that six kings have occupied the royal seat in only four years, and the position is vacant. An elder urges inaction; "Respite," he says, "should do our body politic some good." Orua, he says, needs to "wash / Ourselves completely clean and so dislodge death that / Now / Sits the permanent occupant of our throne." The warrior councilors will not be deterred, however, and they call on Ozidi to speak.

The reluctant hero, with great formality, addresses the four warriors, each by name and praise name, thus defining them as well as identifying his somewhat distant pose. He then admits that the kingship lies with his family, the seventh district of Orua. But all his family are dead except himself and his elder, but unfit, brother. This is the informational crux upon which the opening depends. Ozidi rejects the position for himself and his brother, but Temugedege, the brother, "dribbling with drink," enters and enthusiastically accepts "the royal throne." The crowd responds to the drums and horns and sing "Temugedege ebu gha"--which apparently means "Temugedege is no good" (cf. Ozidi, 31 and Saga, 396; gha is a negation), and dance him off in a grand dance celebration, completing the first scene of the play.

It is thoroughly engaging drama, and would certainly play well if acted. The narrator-protagonist is believable and charming, easily the most attractive character Clark has created. The Council are not greatly differentiated, but there is little reason they should be. All are arrogant and obstinate in the face of the elder's reasonableness and Ozidi's good sense. The principal problem the reader has in conceiving them is their praise names. Ofe the Short is no problem, and Azezabife the Skeleton Man is not much more difficult. Oguaran the Man of Twenty Toes and Twenty Fingers is more difficult, however, and Agbogidi the Nude defies stage convention. Still, the doubling of the one's extremities and the nakedness of the other could be suggested rather than made literal--and should doubtless be so imagined. Thus while the characters are not individually interesting, the behavior and costume of each give implicit excitement and color to the performance.

The scene, besides the crucial action of the choice of king, has a secondary motif: death. Nothing is said to indicate why so many kings have died so quickly, nor how Ozidi's district was all but wiped out. Yet these are the reasons the crisis has arisen. Later in the play, it is revealed to Ozidi's son that "by one stroke of the small-pox king / This whole place, constituting / The seventh district of the city / Of Orua, was in one season / Of no rain burnt to the ground" (Ozidi, 57). This in turn anticipates the ending of the play when the Small-pox King, in anger at being called "Yaws," swears never to return. This is certainly an eventuality greatly to be desired, and in the Saga Ozidi achieves the same end by actually killing the king (Saga, 386). In the Saga, however, there is no suggestion of smallpox as a factor in the precedent death. Clark has provided a tenuous but unifying motif for his play, a motif not found in his sources. Why he did so will be discussed in the next section of this chapter.

The remainder of the first act works out the death of Ozidi. Briefly, Temugedege is a king without honor or tribute. There is a hint in the first scene that the king has a priestly function; Temugedege, however, seems to imagine his role purely as one of luxury and indulgence. When he gets nothing he complains to Ozidi, who is forced by circumstances to challenge the

people. The frightened citizens appeal to Ofe. He
maliciously recalls that a human head is the king's
tribute. Ozidi goes out to join the raid for the head
after a scene with his wife Orea that recalls similar
scenes in Shakespeare's Troilus and Cressida and
Julius Caesar, scenes in which omens and warnings
accurately foretell evil. It is, of course, Ozidi's
head the four warrior councilors have decided to take.
They do so after a momentary difficulty in that they
lack a charm to break the magic protection Ozidi possesses against blade or bullet (Ozidi, 22). The dis-
traught Orea provides the charm, and Ofe presents the
head to Temugedege.

The act ends with preparation for the rest of the
play, the revenge of the hero Ozidi. Orea, contemplating suicide, learns that she is pregnant with a son.
She is then spirited away to the town of her mother,
the great witch Oreame.

The first act is fully one-fourth of the play. This
fact contrasts strongly with the relative brevity of
the same action in The Ozidi Saga. There, 12 out of
390 pages deal with the crisis that is the base for the
whole story. Clark's artistic instinct seems right,
however. Instead of the Saga, he has followed the
festival drama, in which nearly three of its seven days
are needed to complete the action parallel to this
first act. Clark's dramatic action is effective and
sustained. Emotional feeling is high, and a good base
is set for the revenge that will take place in Act
Three. Clark has recognized that an audience needs to
have its sympathy engaged. The elder Ozidi must be a
hero worthy of revenge, and his murderers shown suffi-
ciently despicable to merit the avenging sword. The
Saga audience, however, brought up in admiration of
the hero Ozidi, could be content if these factors were
merely alluded to.

For a similar reason Clark has made the hero's
mother into a character far more significant than the
Orea of the Saga. This is essential because in the
play (as perhaps in the festival) Orea controls the
ending: it is she who treats her son for Yaws, offend-
ing the Small-pox King. (In the Saga she makes the
same wrong diagnosis but neither is the king offended
nor does Orea provide the therapy. At the end, as
throughout, she is a minor figure.) The loving mother
who saves her son through innocence is far more affect-

ing than the Saga's Oreame, who is tainted by cruelty and saves Ozidi so that he can once again fight and kill.

The language of the first act is a loosely marked verse that shows Clark's characteristic modes of dramatic rhetoric. Especially marked is "indirection," familiar from its use in Song of a Goat. Because the vehicles in these figures derive from the river environment, they intensify the reader's sense of place and time. "Are we houseflies," Azezabife asks when the warriors are indecisive about the murder of Ozidi, "That cannot assemble a session of court? / . . . We have agreed upon the act / That will make or mar our joint canoe / Of life. Must we ourselves now capsize / The craft?" (Ozidi, 23). Much more striking is the frightened remark of a citizen contemplating the consequences of making Temugedege king:

> You all know a god is
> A god once you make him so. After
> The ceremony, he ceases to be mere wood. Give him
> Palm oil then, and he'll insist on blood.
> (Ozidi, 15)

It is effective poetry—and good anthropology as well.

The act has set a tone for the entire play, a tone that reflects in English something of the festival mood seen in the film and evident in the Saga. The tone is far from the high seriousness that some readers associate with epic. Clark's own lightly mocking irony hovers ever near, occasionally showing itself, as when the narrator prays to the river gods, "Give us good children," and then goes on satirically,

> and give us good money too.
> After all, in Lagos, Benin, Ibadan, Enugu and
> Kaduna we hear people are now running into streams
>   of riches right up to
> Their necks. Men that yesterday were only teachers,
> Depending on schoolboy collections and firewood,
> Or shoemakers peeling their own soles to eat
> Are today ministers of state riding in cars as big
>   as ships.

It seems more than coincidence that at the time the play was written a notoriously extravagant Federal

Minister, who was like Clark a Mid-Westerner, matched the described characteristics. He had been a school proprietor and, while in office, started a shoe factory. (He was assassinated the same year <u>Ozidi</u> was published and he is alluded to in <u>Casualties</u>; see next chapter.)

Temugedege's opening to the second scene is a simpler irony; properly imagined, it should be hilarious. It is a soliloquy spoken by the foolish "king" with his chewing stick busy in his mouth:

>Now am I king,
>King Temugedege of Orua, terror of all our
>Territories beyond these creeks and
>Keeper of our common store of wealth.

He is generally a thoroughly comic character, an elaboration of the brief sketch in the <u>Saga</u> (<u>Saga</u>, 3). Ofe's decision to bring Temugedege his brother's head as tribute is an ironic gesture also elaborated from the <u>Saga</u> (<u>Saga</u>, 5). He figured prominently in the festival drama, but is not seen in the film.

The drama of the act is inherent; the situation as Clark develops it creates its own tension. The tone undercuts the tension, continually reminding the reader that the story is festive, the motive delight. Overall, the first act is so successful that it fairly demands production. It should be seen, performed by living actors. Unfortunately, the remainder of the play seems to preclude performance of the text as published.

The Central Three Acts. Production difficulties make the succeeding acts difficult to visualize as practical theater. It is, for example, easy enough to imagine a game in which boys shoot arrows at a plantain stalk whirled at the end of a string. It is easy as well to imagine an arrow hitting the stalk. What is more difficult is solving the practical problem of staging the scene with real people, real arrows, a real stalk, and one boy hitting the stalk every time. Yet that is called for in the opening stage direction for the first scene. In the fifth scene, Bouakarakarabiri is seen asleep, standing on his head, feet in the air. When spoken to by Ozidi he somersaults and grabs Ozidi by the neck, using his feet to throttle the boy. Later he puts into his pots three huge animals, a lizard, an

The Ozidi Complex 111

eagle hornbill, and a monkey to create a charm which Ozidi drinks. Again, it is all easy to imagine, but not as practical staging.

An ingenious director, skilled in costume, properties, mime, and dance, could create something of the effects desired, but the task is, without the addition of extensive narration, intimidating. In a large measure, it seems that Clark has written into literal stage directions what Okabou only described and Erivini evoked through costume, mime, and commentary. Clark apparently chose to leave production problems in the practical theater for producers to solve. The result is, inintentionally perhaps, a play for the armchair.

One reason for the complex stage directions is the magic of Oreame, the great witch whose task it is to train her daughter's son for the revenge he must take on the warriors who murdered his father. Oreame in a blink can transform herself into a hill or a leopard to frighten the child Ozidi, as a pretext to shame him for cowardice. Thereafter, as he grows in courage and manhood, she takes him to the wizard Bouakarakarabiri for the lizard-hornbill-monkey "mortar and pestle charm" that gives him rage for battle, and for a charm to make him unpierceable by sword or bullet. Then, when he achieves recognition of his identity as Ozidi, she takes him to a blacksmith for his seven-pronged sword that cries like the bullroarer of a night masquerade as he waves it. At that point he is a man and ready for the revenge he will take in the third act. It is all difficult staging at best.

For the third and fourth acts he has a retinue. Besides mother and grandmother, he is accompanied by a personal slave, a sword bearer, a horn blower, and several drummers. The musicians will accompany each of his battles, urging him on and celebrating his victories. Here Clark has followed a tradition that may be relevant to the origin of the epic. Wrestling was since time forgotten the most popular of sports in the delta, competitions being great affairs, musical as well as physical. One aspect of the Ozidi story is here illuminated: Ozidi is the town champion, elevated to epic powers. The murderers of the elder Ozidi are the young wrestler's domestic challengers, and the other, later, monsters are the strangers Orua's champion must overcome to the town's honor and renown.

Ozidi with his retinue in the play returns to Orua and learns for himself the identity of the murderers. The murderers learn of his coming, and he fights Azezabife and Ofe. His other fights are summarized in a stage direction (Ozidi, 79). With the end of the act, the vengeance is complete. The fourth act involves Ozidi in the gratuitous adventures, against alien monsters.

The most striking aspect of the central three acts is the energy and power of Oreame. She takes the boy Ozidi, transforms him into man and hero, saves him when he verges on defeat, and finally falls victim to the frenzy her own herb has caused in her grandson. She is victim of her own actions since she has personally enlisted the supernatural powers that he both possesses and is possessed by. Clark has set her in continual contrast with her gentle daughter Orea. Orea urges both Oreame and Ozidi to moderation and is always refused. This is natural because Oreame represents the active principle in the hero and also because she is co-agent with Ozidi of divine justice.

Tamara, God Almighty, is Oreame's strong backer so long as Ozidi pursues his vengeance. When Oreame prays to Her, She replies in thunder (Ozidi, 75-76), and when Ozidi is helpless before the attack of Ofe, Tamara's thunder intervenes so that Ozidi is refreshed while Ofe succumbs to charms Tamara has ordered Oreame to put before him (Ozidi, 87). But Tamara abandons the great witch after she has virtually forced Ozidi to murder a mother and child (and after he has murdered a woman who used sex in an effort to discover his "secret," Ozidi, 110). Oreame had no charm against her own grandson.

Oreame's fate is purely Clark's invention. Nothing happens to her in Erivini's version, and Okabou in the Saga allows Ozidi to kill her so that she can demonstrate her vast powers by coming to him in a dream and teaching him how to bring her back to life (Saga, 310-11). The Saga provided only a hint of retributive justice, but Clark apparently found it irresistible for his drama, and again his artistic judgment seems sound, as will be shown in greater detail later. The horrors of Ozidi's cruelty must be paid for somehow (in the English tradition if not the Ijọ) and only Oreame is a suitable scapegoat. Clark has not made her--or any other character except Orea--endearing, so

she justly fails, with scarcely an empathetic pang.
The action of the play is intrinsically too grotesque for audience empathy to be likely. Clark's comedy and irony both further distance audience and character, while increasing pleasure. Two characters are especially delightful, Ozidi's comic servant and Ewiri the Amananaowei of Orua. Omoni, the servant, has no counterpart in Clark's sources; he is, however, a parallel to the blacksmith in the Saga who is funny because of his bad Ijo (he is an Igbo from Awka, famous for its ironworkers). Omoni speaks pidgin English which, when set in contrast to standard, always evokes sophisticated laughter. Omoni is the common "bush" man, credulous, fearful, and, like the poor everywhere, a bit cynical.

(Readers unfamiliar with pidgin have trouble with Omoni's lines. His first line is opaque: "Massa, papa kuku leaf shed for market sef?" Yet the meaning is simple, "Master, did your father leave you a market shed?" Ozidi replies that his father's business was the state. This evokes a cynical and anachronistic observation about public servants who do not forget to get rich--like the girl who eats most of the food she is supposed to give the baby in her care. Omoni further wants to know why "mama"--Oreame--sent them to the market to discover the means of the elder Ozidi's death, since he left no stall tenant who would have the information. And he becomes fearful when Ozidi proposes to wait at the branching of the road: "Hey, massa, nor si'don for dis kine place, oh! Na for here spirits day fly. Plenty people way you day see for market na proper spirit from watah, nor be man-pickin at all at all." In this he reflects a common idea that at crossroads lurk spirits--in Ijo lands, of course, they are water spirits--and in large markets these spirits disguise themselves as "man-pickin," mortals, in order to lure more people to destruction or captivity. When Ozidi has learned the truth, Omoni is appalled: "But una country people dey do wicked oh!"--una meaning "your" (Ozidi, 66-67, 71).

Ewiri is less funny and far more cynical. He is the embodiment of Ewiri the "trickster tortoise" of a thousand folk tales. With light heart he brings the murderers the news that the avenging Ozidi has come, and, when only Ofe is left, Ewiri cheerfully recites to him the fate of his companions. He is most trickster

of all when he falsely reports to Ozidi that Tebesonoma
has challenged him, and then takes a similar message to
Tebesonoma (as in a popular folk tale; see chapter 1).
  The fight is itself an excess, and it leads to the
one scene that borders on the sentimental and climaxes
in Ozidi's worst excess of all. Tebesonoma, dying,
warns Ozidi to kill his sister and her son lest they
avenge in their good time. The sister is as innocent
as her child, and is sweetly hospitable. Ozidi rebels
against the murder but Oreame is relentless. It is, of
course, this crime that Clark establishes, indirectly,
as the reason Oreame must die.
  The Last Act; Commentary. The fifth act is a con-
tinuous action with two interlinked locations, one the
beach where Engarando the Smallpox King lands his
barge, and the other is Ozidi's house. In the latter
Ozidi sickens, and Engarando's servants, Cold, Head-
ache, Spots, and Fever, afflict him. Orea invokes
Tamara. In the midst of her prayer she recalls that
Ozidi has never suffered yaws, and she immediately
begins treating him for that common childhood skin
disease. Engarando indignantly declares he will go and
never return. He departs to brisk music that leads to
a procession with Ozidi at its head, triumphant at last
without violence.
  Although Clark is not precise on the subject, it
seems that "the Smallpox King goes off in a huff" in
Erivini's version (Saga, xxiii) as in the play; the
film of Erivini's performance shows very clearly
Engarando's barge, described in the play as "a party
of players in a double dance formation representing the
moving barge" (Ozidi, 115). This illustrates
Clark's contention that in the play he "treated the
combined accounts of the Ozidi myth . . . just as
Shakespeare in his Roman and English plays handled
history. . . ." Clark used what he saw fit, omitted
most of what he had available, and added what he
thought he needed. The result is not so much melange
as one might expect. Adequately imagined, it suggests
the festive drama rather well.
  The play thus is a mixed thing. Clark let his materials dominate his art, while imposing alien language
and form on his materials. The struggle shows: the
play is forced and awkward. Yet at the same time it is
marvelously good reading. Clark's errors in language
(see below) are too rare to be intrusive, and his

poetic felicity remains high. As T. S. Eliot said of
Hamlet, Ozidi is an artistic failure. But it is
continually interesting; it has form, and one finishes
reading it with a sense of satisfying completeness.
Ozidi, arising from sickness, fully alive, leads the
grand procession of performers and spectators alike.
The reader would be happy to join them.

Ozidi: Festival as Belles Lettres

In writing the play, Clark had as a major objective
making available to a national and international reading public an authentic African artistic and dramatic
experience. In two essays, "The Legacy of Caliban" and
"Aspects of Nigerian Drama," both published in The
Example of Shakespeare (1970), Clark has indicated
some of the factors he took into account in order to
preserve authenticity while creating a new work of
belles lettres. Before examining in detail what
Clark did in fact do, it would be well to examine the
prior factors as Clark has identified them.

Briefly, Clark's initial objective was to achieve a
high degree of verisimilitude. He had, to begin with,
a traditional art form, the drama, which had certain
coincidences and correspondence with European forms.
These similarities could be exploited. He could, for
example, blend the English language with African
music--including drum, song, and dance--and with the
narrative action. At the same time, he could use
English while establishing clear verbal distinction
from English tradition through the use of images and
themes appropriate to the time, place, and characters
(Example, 17, 21, 83, 86, 23). Central to Clark's
method is the principle of decorum. The language,
though alien, must nevertheless correspond accurately
with the character, his role in society, his education
in relation to other characters, his culture. Verisimilitude, the primary objective, is to be achieved
through the suitability of each element in the drama to
the time, the place, the situation, the history, the
world of the play.

It should not be supposed that such verisimilitude
is a simple matter. As Clark has shown at length, European writers have done poorly in their attempts to
achieve verisimilitude. Naturalism, the obvious choice
of style, proves upon examination (of Defoe and Cary,

among other English writers) to be seriously, even grotesquely, misleading. Shakespeare, Clark shows, provides the better example: Caliban, Aaron, and Othello use no "dialect" of English; their alien character is established through imagery and diction (<u>Example</u>, 6-17). The example of Shakespeare is the best example, and Clark chooses to follow it. Nevertheless as a twentieth-century African dramatist he is in no position to follow that example readily. The artist is, first of all, himself, and of his own age. His experience is his own, and his assimilation of experience, as well as his molding of it to an artistic purpose is unique. And, very significantly, each artist has an audience of his own (<u>Example</u>, 18).

Clark's audience is vast and complex. It is neither sixteenth-century London nor twentieth-century Ij<u>o</u>. It is no less than the whole contemporary English-speaking world. Further, the English-speaking world is possessed of sophisticated means of ordering experience artistically. These means correspond only coincidentally to African means. Clark's objective, the achievement of decorum through imagery and theme, is thus a complex task, inevitably somewhat at odds with the achievement of verisimilitude, yet indispensable to it.

A paradox results: to be true to the Ij<u>o</u> originals, and yet communicate truly in English to an English-speaking audience, Clark must be false to the Ij<u>o</u>. So stated, the paradox is beyond resolution, yet the play <u>Ozidi</u> somehow seems to succeed. Its success justifies the critic in reviewing how so much apparent Ij<u>o</u> truth is evoked in spite of--or perhaps with the aid of--the distortion glass of English rhetoric, which has little in common with the rhetoric of Ij<u>o</u>.

Clark had both the <u>Saga</u> and Erivini's festive drama as bases for his play. Now, the rhetoric of the <u>Saga</u> is not only not like English rhetoric, it is also a world apart from the festive drama. The rhetoric of Erivini's drama is, first of all, nonverbal. Its form is mime, music, song, and dance. The drama is spectacular: costumes, masks, makeup, weapons, ritual paraphernalia, and properties embellish the action, mixing symbol and actuality (see <u>Example</u>, 86-87). These are wholly acceptable modes of dramatic rhetoric, but they are not modes of the <u>Saga</u>. On the other hand there are correspondences between the <u>Saga</u> narrator <u>O</u>kabou

and the festival actor Erivini in performance. Both
narrate--on vastly different scales, of course--and
both assume roles: both are actors, as is the narrator-
hero of the play. Both interact with the audience.
This interaction, Clark indirectly observes, is an
essential of Ijo rhetoric, along with music and some
degree of emotional engagement. That engagement may be
extreme--to the point of actual "possession" in the
drama (Example, 87).

In transforming Ozidi from festive-epic-drama into
an English play, Clark was forced to give up some vital
precedent Ijo rhetorical forms and a great part of
the narrative. "Possession," for example, may be
called for in a stage direction, and the reader may
imagine it, if such a thing be imaginable for him, but
it no longer directly influences behavior. It is no
longer part of the rhetoric of the drama. Gone too is
the spontaneous interaction of performer and audience: Clark's play text calls for only a moment or two
of spectator participation (Ozidi, 2-4 perhaps, and
the final procession, 121).

The language of the Saga could lend little to the
play. The Saga's rhetorical modes are incantatory,
onomatopoetic, repetitive, responsive, musical, descriptive, hyperbolic, and magical. The diction of the
Saga is literal, not metaphorical (though it contains
metaphors). This last point is a central consideration
here and will be dealt with at some length after the
lesser rhetorical contrasts have been shown.

One rhetorical contrast in some measure dominates
the others. The film of the festive drama and the
transcription of the Saga are both recordings of
performances. The printed play is not. In this,
Ozidi differs from most drama in which the printed
version has been extensively revised from an original
author's script, revised in the pressure of rehearsal
and, often, revised further during and after performance. As was shown earlier, indicated actions in Ozidi
often seem impossible, and the relation between what is
said and what the audience is presumed to be seeing is
often obscure. The play, like the festive drama, includes music, mime, dance, and song, and, like the
Saga, miracles, but the bare printed text leaves
these modes as suggestions only. For example, in Act
Four, Scene Two, a stage direction reads, "They fight.
Ozidi's cauldron music fills the place. He crops off

six heads from Tebesonoma, one after the other." For Okabou, such an event was easily told. How (and if) it was performed by Erivini does not appear in the film. The play producer has a practical problem. He must show something. He would probably not attempt a literal representation; the complexity is too great. Yet a presentational action--mimed, symbolic--would be difficult to effect clearly and would seem out of place when Tebesonoma rather literally completes the action by falling on his knees to beg that his remaining (chicken) head be spared.

To escape the problems of such stage directions and indicated actions, the critic is obliged to attempt to understand the play as dramatic poetry rather than as a text for performance. The critic then must concentrate on the dialogue, to find (as in a play by Shakespeare, as usually read) the play's meanings and values in the words characters speak. The music, dance, song, and mime are less relevant, unseen and unheard, and the dominant rhetoric of the play is to be discovered through the language.

When this is done, the nonverbal festive drama and the verbal play text nevertheless still have much in common. Overall they share a narrative action. Clark, as was noticed earlier, preserved the narrator-hero and the ritual invocation of the water spirits. These are both rhetorical modes seen in the film. The week-long festival is condensed, however, into five relatively brief acts. Temugedege in both versions becomes king, and the envious town leaders ambush Ozidi to present his head to his unfortunate king-brother. Thereafter the play and drama narrations are roughly parallel. Oreame, or as in the play, another woman, a fellow witch, tells Ozidi's wife, Orea, Oreame's daughter, that she is pregnant. Oreame thereafter rears the new Ozidi, testing him until his courage is certain. She gets him his sword and sets him to trap the wives of his father's murderers. In the festival (as in the Saga), Ozidi kills the wives, but in the play Ozidi merely half bares their bodies to incite their anger. Earlier in the play (later in the festival; Saga, 406) Ozidi has acquired a charm whose ingredients cry out in his bowels, and he conquers all his enemies. In somewhat different order, varying with the version, Ozidi fights Tebesonoma and Odogu, and then, in fights omitted from the play, kills many more monsters before encountering the Smallpox King. In both dramatic ver-

The Ozidi Complex

sions treatment for yaws insults the Smallpox King, who departs, leaving Ozidi alive with—it appears—no further battles to fight.

Such a narrative can be conveyed in action, with narrative as a mere "programme sheet," as Clark has called Erivini's text (Saga, xv). The action's rhetorical development in the English language—a contrast to Erivini's performance—is wholly new, incorporating elements derived from the Saga as well as Clark's own inventions. It is not easy to define securely what has been taken from the Saga in many instances because the film is the only evidence for the festival: an event in the Saga but not in the film nevertheless may have been in the festival; the seven festival days are condensed to a forty-five-minute film. Clark however has said that the Okabou text is both better shaped and fuller than the others (Saga, xv-xvii). The assumption is therefore reasonable that, in any given example, a play element found in the Saga but not in the film is derived from the Saga. Play elements found in neither film nor Saga may reasonably be taken as Clark's invention.

One example can illustrate both derivation and invention. Night Five of the Saga follows the killing of Ofe and opens with Ozidi's confrontation with the Amananaowei of Orua, called "king" (cf. Saga, 208, and note 3, 268). Ozidi then meets and decapitates the Scrotum King, has a flirtation with Odogu's wife, is captured by Tebesonoma, gets free, reluctantly kills Tebesonoma's sister and her new-born child, and finally dispatches Tebesonoma, to end the night's tale. In Act Four of the play, the Amananaowei again appears, as Ewiri, the trickster tortoise. Clark, in the play, has Ewiri quietly overhear Ozidi tell of his fight with the Scrotum King. Then Ewiri—a chatty, hungry fellow, adept at getting food and drink—interprets Ozidi's dream as evidence the hero needs a wife. He then goes on to amuse himself with a simple trickster-tortoise lie, telling Ozidi that Tebesonoma has determined to fight. Ozidi of course sets a challenge. Ewiri, completing his trick, carries the challenge to Tebesonoma. He has thus tricked them both into unsought battle (Ozidi, 99). Ozidi kills Tebesonoma. Then, to prevent revenge, he must go on to kill the sister and nephew. Afterwards he flirts with and kills Odogu's wife (an act which leads to the play's climax in Scene Five of Act Four).

A rhetorical transformation has been achieved through Ewiri. The trickster adds a surprise and reversal to a somewhat monotonous succession of battles. Clark's invention here is pure dramatic rhetoric. Ozidi has opened the act complaining of his discontent now that he has no further revenge to seek; his dream of the Scrotum King is a nightmare. Ewiri's voice (in a refreshing change of tone) is graceful and charming-- and clever and deceitful as well. He extends the Ozidi-Orea domestic scene, suggesting (as the Saga does not) that Ozidi may have hope of a peaceful domestic life. By his tricking Ozidi into the fight with Tebesonoma and by inciting the hero to seek out a woman, Ewiri becomes a mechanism for the production of new adventures. In the Saga, Ozidi fights on merely because there are other enemies to fight. In the play, Ozidi must be provoked. As will be seen later, this change is related to the metaphorical nature of the play as a whole and is central to Clark's transformation from the literal narrative.

A very different rhetorical device is the pidgin speech of Ozidi's servant in Act Three, Scene Three. As was pointed out earlier, there is no direct precedent in the Saga, so the diction must be seen as pure invention even though the pidgin serves a purpose paralleled in the Saga. In Night One, the maker of Ozidi's sword is an "Ibo" blacksmith--an Igbo who "speaks bad Ibo" and not very good Ijo (Saga, 42- 45, notes 41 and 47; 58). The function served in each case, the Igbo blacksmith and Ozidi's servant, is to widen the geographical scope of the action: Ozidi lives in a world that has extension. Servant or blacksmith, an alien speaks in an alien tongue. Pidgin English would be absurd in an Ijo tale, but in an English play, the pidgin is rhetorically exact: it delineates the relationship of the two men (cf. Example, 92). The blacksmith in the play of course speaks perfect English. The reason is obvious: there is no useful dialectical variation of English to distinguish between the speech of Igbo Awka and Ijo Orua (Ozidi, 52).

Less felicitous are several minor points of diction that might be noted, evident concessions to the English language and its cultural heritage (e.g., the fable of the tortoise and the hare, Ozidi, 41, or a metaphorical fire-breathing dragon, 57). Unforgivable is

Ewiri's appreciation of Ozidi's hospitality: "Who said a good wine / Needs no bush?" Ozidi should, but does not, answer "Shakespeare." Such usage is not successful because it does not accord with Clark's own urging that appropriate language will "delineate the contour and colour of one given setting as against another" (Example, 23). Such lapses are to be mentioned only because they contrast with other European rhetorical modes that enrich the play's diction, through entirely appropriate language.

Mentioned earlier is what Clark calls "indirection." The master of this technique is Ewiri, especially in Act Three, Scene Two, when he brings to the murderers of the elder Ozidi the ghastly news that his avenger has come to Orua. "Are you," he asks in pretended innocence, "sitting there drinking palm-wine when pepper / Has fallen in the fire before you?" When at length the drinkers penetrate Ewiri's riddles, they reply in kind: "Did you say the cock has laid an egg?" (Ozidi, 62, 65). What makes the technique exciting is the union of an English ironic jest with a homely riddle, in diction localized to the time, place, and culture.

A variation on the technique of "indirection" has also been seen before, the brief, aphoristic parable, as when the fearful Agbogidi begins to regret his hand in the murder: "The sacrifice of a son of the soil / To his ancestors is a long rope / Without end . . ." (Ozidi, 65). Or again, Ofe's reply, "If first we look for a stick / Long enough, we shall never kill the snake / In the house" (Ozidi, 66). Neither this nor the preceding are readily translated to or from the Ijo. Indeed, Clark's translation of the Saga implies that such techniques are not common in that language. But they are legitimate representations of states of mind, whether English or Ijo. They convey to the reader the impression of verisimilitude: if these characters speak in English, this is precisely the English they would speak--granted initially that they are characters in a drama and not ordinary men. (Verisimilitude in drama, it must be remembered, does not require Hamlet or Stanley Kowalski to speak as anyone else does; each exists on his own level of rhetoric.)

Some levels or modes of rhetoric are, as has been implied earlier, beyond diction, or transcend it. The greatest of rhetorical figures is allegory, which may be mimed, spoken, or pictured. Through it the universal can be seen in the particular. The play Hamlet, for example, is an allegory of divine justice--justice that crushes the guilty in their crimes and then sends flights of angels to speed the agent of justice to his rest. Ozidi too is allegorical. Clark has required that Ozidi should display, at the least, retributive justice. In his "Introductory Essay" to the Saga, Clark analyzed the variants among the narratives. "The most significant," he said, "concerns the excesses committed by Ozidi." He kills the sister and new-born nephew of Tebesonoma and then "goes on to commit crimes against himself." He kills his uncle Temugedege. "Then he performs the ultimate [in the Saga] by almost murdering the supreme sorceress herself, his grandmother Oreame, who is his mainstay." In these crimes Clark finds "natural law and justice, the self-consumptive process of justice, especially when pursued with power that recognizes no other sanction than itself." This natural law and justice are found in the Okabou text alone, Clark says (Saga, xvi-xvii).

It was seen that even in the Okabou text Oreame is finally undefeated; her death is temporary. In the Saga she comes in a dream to tell Ozidi that the herb needed is easily found. He finds it, and, first anointing his sword with it, he again attacks her, this time bringing her to life (Saga, 310-14). Thus she lives on to see Ozidi through his last great battle, his violent conquest of the Smallpox King.

Clark grants her no such salvation in the play. To do so would preclude a just retribution for her incitement of Ozidi to criminal excess. If Okabou knew he was dealing retributive justice through his narrative, there is no sign of that knowledge in the translated text of the Saga. But Clark's play is metaphorical, not literal: his allegory requires suffering. Ozidi goes berserk and in an almost simultaneous action kills his enemy Odogu and his beloved mentor Oreame. Both die finally and permanently (Ozidi, 114).

The Saga is all but free of suffering. Orea, it is true, laments the death of her husband, and Temugedege laments for his brother (Saga, 110), but both laments are shortlived, and Oreame swiftly gives Orea protection and then adds the comforting assurance that she bears a child. Temugedege's lament, like his moral character, amounts to little. These laments (and occasional others) are examples of the Saga's rhetorical diversity, but are not central to the tone of the whole. More characteristic is the comic narrative quoted earlier of the slaying of Azeza's wife in the Saga: when she is sliced, she rushes out "all pieces cutting through the air"--or, in the Ijo, "O, Azeza ta wan duo para para para para para para pa pa pa pa pa / vou vou vou vou vou" (Saga, 55). Comic onomatopoesis is triumphant. Again, Ozidi, typically unsuffering, murders his uncle Temugedege merely because he doesn't like the old man, and the account of the killing stirs laughter in the spectators (Saga, 372-75). In short, the Saga exhausts its moral base when Ozidi's revenge for his father's murder is complete with the death of Ofe at the end of Night Four. The three remaining nights of the Saga display an Ozidi whose only discontent is lack of slaughter when, as rarely happens, he has none to do. The Saga unquestionably has a multitude of purposes of high social value, but no European moral aesthetic purpose is served: the Saga, like the festive drama, has no allegory. It is less painful than a series of wrestling matches. It is the kind of story a hero tale should be, exciting and entertaining.

On the other hand, Clark's own allegorical Ozidi suffers. Long before he kills his grandmother, he is wracked, like Macbeth, by terrible dreams:

> Oh yes, my father, all set up now and free from
>   the grove of night
> Sleeps well indeed, while I walk here awake, for
> I have only to close my eyes and heads of those
> I have slaughtered tumble forth, rolling and
> Hopping about my feet like huge jiggers
> Screaming to suck my blood.
>   (Ozidi, 91)

Required by Oreame to kill Tebesonoma's sister, he cries out in desperation, "Let me be! I don't want to kill anybody again" (Ozidi, 105). Oreame persists, and Ozidi proceeds in killing until his mother Orea, seeing him kill Odogu's wife, cries in her anguish,

> Leave the woman alone, Ozidi!
> Now is there nothing else you can do but kill?

Oh, no more sleep for us again in this house.
(Ozidi, 111)

Ozidi's blind slaughters of Odogu and Oreame swiftly follow.

Orea, Ozidi's mother, so prominent in Clark's play, is present in the Saga but slight in her effect. In the play, Clark has given her profound metaphorical significance. She is innocence, allegorized. In the introduction to the Saga, Clark asserts that Ozidi is saved "at last in spite of himself only through the innocence of his mother and the purity of ordinary water" (Saga, xvi-xvii). It must be presumed that he is describing the action of the festive drama. Although in the Saga Orea initially mistakes smallpox for yaws (Saga, 379), Oreame (not Orea) swiftly goes for a cure. It is not water, but medicine which, mixed with water, she uses to wash Ozidi's festering flesh (Saga, 381-84), healing him. Healed, Ozidi sweeps to slaughter, chopping up the Smallpox King, his men, and even his boat (Saga, 386). Afterwards, Ozidi cries out the names of both Orea and Oreame, calling each, "my mother" (Saga, 386-88). In contrast, Clark ends the play with Orea washing her son's body with common water and soap. This leads to the Smallpox King's furious departure.

The exit of the Smallpox King awakens Ozidi to the triumphant procession that concludes the play. Ozidi's last battle has been fought with soap, not a sword, and the hero, cleansed, is at last free to live simply as a man among men. The stability of society is restored. The play is over, concluded, unified, aesthetically satisfying. This completion has been made possible by the new rhetoric of allegory, the ultimate metaphor.

The supernatural base for the allegory is an elaboration, from hints in the Saga, of the role of "Oyin the Mother or Tamara, She Who is the Moulder of All," as Clark identifies her (Saga, xxiv). Tamara has no active role in the Saga, but in the play she is invoked at least nine times (Ozidi, 21, 25, 31, 38, 40, 75, 76, 87, 117, 119), four times by Orea and three by Oreame. Orea prays that Ozidi not be killed and that she not be left without child. Tamara grants the second, only half of her wish (Ozidi, 21, 31). It is a Delphic irony. On the other hand, Oreame's prayer to Tamara for Ozidi's success in revenge is wholly granted (Ozidi, 75-76). At the end Tamara inspires the Small-

pox King to his "huff," in response to Orea's prayer
(Ozidi, 119-20). Invocation of the Goddess gives
order to the allegory, satisfying the conception that
divine providence has both will and means to achieve
justice.

A final theme developed by Clark to give new rhetorical unity to the dramatic narrative combines the Smallpox King's own cruelty with the cleansing of Orua that ensures the people's freedom from the disease. The theme is hinted rather than developed. The need for cleansing is stressed early in the play by an elder who, like Antony's Old Soldier in Shakespeare's play, pleads wisely but ineffectually. His plea is that Orua

> Go and find how we may wash
> Ourselves completely clean and so dislodge death that
> Now
> Sits permanent occupant of our throne.
>
> (Ozidi, 6-7)

Six kings in "four floods have died," he says, and Ozidi later adds that of his "teeming section of the town," "Death has left just me and my brother" (Ozidi, 9). The killer is smallpox. Ozidi's widow later explains:

> by one stroke of the small-pox king
> This whole place, constituting
> The seventh district of the city
> Of Orua, was in one season
> Of no rain burnt to the ground.
>
> (Ozidi, 57)

Smallpox, then, is the ultimate enemy. The murderers of the elder Ozidi and the monsters Ozidi conquers in Act Four are scattered individuals. Smallpox first destabilized the body politic. Destabilized, Orua chose to proclaim an idiot king. Then Orua must at last be cleansed from smallpox. The means is through Orea's innocence, and the result is that Ozidi arises triumphant, Orua's hero.

Clark may have imagined or sensed that, in some past generation, a legend had a clearly developed theme, the hero cleansing the world from its enemy, smallpox. In time that cleansing tale, by accretion and mutation, became part of the Ozidi tale, a final scrap of violence with which Okabou ends his recitation. The point is not arguable (7). Such an origin is neither probable nor especially improbable. But the cleansing is meaningful in the play. The departure of Engarandon the Smallpox King is doubly an occasion for joy. Not only is Ozidi spared a loathsome death, but Orua is forever freed from the disease. Engarandon cries,

> The mortal wretch called us Yaws to our royal face.
> Now hear me all of you: let no member of our train
> Set foot again on this shore where men see
> A royal python and call it worm of the earth . . .
> (Ozidi, 120-21)

As in Oedipus Rex, the plague is lifted from the city. The problem that inaugurated the action has been resolved and a classic unity has been achieved. That unity is missing from the Saga (and perhaps the festival). But, in Clark's play, Ozidi rises to lead all Orua in joyous procession.

The play Ozidi represents, with the film and the Saga (and the recording of Songs from "The Ozidi Saga"), another valid representation of the Ozidi tale. The tale is not immutable, as was shown at the start of this chapter. It was told and performed for generations, time not easily counted today. It has changed before, in the three versions explored by Clark and in many others currently now in the delta. Though transformed by a rhetoric of European origin, the belles lettres version is still a variation of "the Ijo truth."

Conclusion

The Ozidi complex as Clark has recorded and re-created it is a grand, if sometimes ambiguous, achievement. In the play, the film, and the saga an indigenous African epic is preserved and re-created as no other has been. The re-creation is continually exciting, but, more important, it evokes an authentic African experience. The variety of forms provides an unprecedented sense of the whole. Nowhere else can the student, whether African or alien, find so rounded and fully dimensioned a record of what is now a lost experience of epic.

Clark has shown a way for others to follow and perfect. While it is true that others have filmed

The Ozidi Complex

festivals and recorded sagas, none heretofore has attempted an artistic integration of the oral tradition experience on so large, so comprehensive a scale. The attempt is worthy of admiration and emulation.

There are inevitably flaws. Unnoticed in the preceding account are the remarks by critics of Clark's methods, his transcription, and his translation. The film is not so pleasing as it is interesting; it is informative but difficult to follow. The play is certainly spiritually near its models but it is also very close to European models, and its values sometimes seem alien, too.

Doubts should not have the final word. Spectators often cry out to Okabou, "Is it the Ijo thing?" asking confirmation that he has the story right. There is not, nor has there been, a definitive version of Ozidi's tale. Clark's Ozidi complex seems far more to be, than not to be, "the Ijo thing."

Upon completion of his research fellowship at Ibadan, Clark was appointed lecturer at the University of Lagos. He remained on the staff there through the crisis and war that led to the composition of his lyric-narrative collection of poems that he titled <u>Casualties</u>.

Chapter Five
Casualties

Casualties: Poems 1966-68 (1970) has two parts. The first is the one to which the main title specifically refers. The subject of these poems is the Nigerian crisis and civil war. The second part is "Incidental Songs for Several Persons." "Casualties" as an integral whole will be discussed first, with one additional poem first published much later. Discussion of the incidental poems will conclude this chapter.

Casualties: Lyrics of War

The twenty-eight numbered poems of Casualties are the lyric expression of a partially stated narrative. Clark's notes to the poems represent a partial statement of the narrative. The full narrative is two-fold; it contains the whole political history of Nigeria's early years as an independent nation, and it tells the personal history of Clark himself in relation to his friends--friends whom, one way or another, he lost in the troubled years. The lyrics themselves are simple for the most part. Their simplicity, which has deceived some critics, is made possible through symbolic representations of persons and events; the symbols, too, can be deceptive. It is necessary to explicate the major symbols and provide a narrative if the lyrics are to be read in their political and personal context.

The simplicity, and its deceptiveness, are well illustrated in the second poem of the series, "Skulls and Cups." One critic has called this "tepid poetry" in which Clark is "singing (one can hardly say lamenting) the death of his most intimate friends" (1). The poem is far from "tepid"; it is ice cold: "'Look, J.P., / How do you tell a skull / From another?'" it begins, in a rhetorical question attributed to "Obi." He is identified in a note as Dr. Obiajunwa Wali (Casualties, 55). "Obi" goes on to compare the skulls of "Chris," "Sam," and "Emman" to cups: "'How does one tell a cup on the floor / From another, when the spirit

is emptied?'" While Casualties, as a whole, may be
expressive of grief for the loss of friends, "Skulls
and Cups" is not. It is a preliminary poem, a stage
setting as it were, for what is to come. What the
attentive reader needs to see is how carefully the
individuals named in the poem were chosen.

Four of the five persons in the poem rejected or
abandoned support of Eastern Nigeria's 1967 withdrawal
from the federation of Nigeria. Wali, though in the
east at the start of the war, became a Commissioner for
Rehabilitation in a state separated from the east.
"JP"--Clark himself--found fragmentation too great a
danger to Nigeria and declined to join the easterners
(Casualties, 58-59). Of the three "skulls" two,
Emmanuel Ifeajuna and Sam Agbam, were easterners who
initially were involved in the secession but then were
themselves executed by the secessionist government,
accused of profederation activities. The fifth was the
poet Christopher Okigbo, to whom Clark was closest and
whose loss Clark felt the most. Okigbo had no opportunity to turn against the secession; he was killed in
the first federal advance.

Indirectly the poem says that, although the poet has
lost his friends, it is not to be presumed that he
betrayed them. As will be seen, Clark later raises the
possibility that Okigbo might have, in time, defected
in the civil war, as his friends were later to do. The
poem--far from a lament--asks that the war and its
waste of lives be seen in context. Each participant
has a history, each event a circumstance, each decision
a conflict. The whole series of poems, based on this
kind of understanding, becomes deeply moving, not as a
lament, but as cumulative experience.

The experience the reader shares is Clark's. It is
not, however, Clark's precisely as he lived it. The
poems are a mask for the poet, and the experiences are
those of the mask. These are the public poems of a
private person and they are shaped in part by the
poet's perception of the public for which he wrote. As
will be seen--as is already known by all who have read
these poems--the experience portrayed in Casualties
is terrible. Many of the poems probably had their
origin close to the time of the events that inspired
them, and all had been written before the time of civil
war had ended. They were written when uncertainty and
death were still large in the land.

It is likely that the "friends" in the opening poem, "Song," and the "faces" in the closing poem, "Night Song," are the collective dead well beyond those specifically identified in Clark's notes, for before the war ended it surely seemed unlikely to him that the casualties among his acquaintances would be so few. "Song" begins,

> I can look the sun in the face
> But the friends that I have lost
> I dare not look at any.

It is a kind of confession. Clark is not innocent, and the state of mind that produced the poems is not innocence. The poems are an <u>apologia</u>, a vindication.

In the patterned structure of <u>Casualties</u>, the friends of "Song" are joined in "Night Song" by "The strange and young I never met" who "intercept the faces I loved" and blot out the sun "that I / believe should ripen the land anew." This expansion to include strangers among the faces indicates the transformation of experience that lies between the two poems, inherent in the submerged narrative. The poems between tell why the poet dares not look, and they imaginatively widen the scope of the poetry beyond the poet's own predicament, to the circumstances of the whole state. (Indeed, the final lines of "Night Song" are optimistic, as will be seen later.) Both "Song" and "Night Song" are written in a continuing present time; present time in the sense that the events of the narrative are already past.

The following discussion of these poems will develop the underlying narrative as the poems imply it should be seen. The narrative should not be read as history, though it includes many facts, and the facts will be as accurate as the available materials permit. But the real history lies in the interpretation of the facts; it lies in which facts are stated and which left out, in the perspective and point of view of the presenter of the facts. Clark has asked, by implication, in the poems and in the notes he appended to them that his experience be seen in a particular way. The narrative in this chapter conforms largely to the perspective and point of view implied in the poems. As a result, it will omit much that would clearly suggest alternative interpretations.

Casualties

For the most part the poems will be taken up in the order in which Clark arranged them. But some, notably "Season of Omens," will be taken out of order for narrative clarity.

The present approach to the poems does not permit strictly literary criticism. As a general comment, however, the reader may note that in Casualties Clark has greatly extended his use of the animal folk tale as metaphor. Most of the poems, in one way or another, use animals as representatives or symbols for actual persons. The contents of the poems are folk tales or fabulous stories which, like the main narrative, are often only partially stated. In the tales the animals are the active participants in political conflict.

Clark is entirely in accord with tradition in thus adapting the folktale technique to political narrative. Satirical application of proverbial tales to current village affairs is ancient custom throughout southern Nigeria (and elsewhere as well; one may recall the political ironies of Mother Goose rhymes in England). Clark has expanded a traditional village form in order to comment on great affairs of state. That the form is naturally ironic suits Clark's purpose very well.

"Song" and "Skull and Cups," while figurative, do not well illustrate the folktale adaptation. Also, they are in present time. But "Skull and Cups" begins a shift back in time (recalling deaths which occurred in the first months of the war), and the third poem, "Vulture's Choice," both makes the profound shift in time to anticipation of the 1966 coup, and simultaneously begins the re-creation of political events through ironic folktale. With "Vulture's Choice" the main narrative and its symbolic evocation may be said to begin.

"Vulture's Choice" has been misread as Clark's assertion "that the Jan. 1966 coup was politically motivated from the outset," with "politically motivated" here meaning that it was an Eastern Nigerian usurpation of power (2). Yet Clark's own note to the poem calls it only a "parable of choice facing the five majors and the country they wanted to save" (Casualties, 55). In the poem Vulture has been married six years, corresponding obviously to Nigeria's 1960-1966 period of independence. Vulture, however, has no child. "Vulture" symbolizes Nigeria's discontented radicals (especially the young officers planning a coup d'etat),

who still awaited the "child," political and economic
independence from the neocolonial power of Europe. In
the parable, Vulture must deal with the inherent dangers of the birth he wants: the child, the mother, or
both may die. Vulture resolves to eat either or both,
for "Six years is a long time / To be married and no
child!" The urgency of these words depends on a sense
of the Nigerian political situation at the start of
1966. To the revolutionaries, continued colonial
control after independence was largely responsible for
the disastrous political condition of Nigeria as 1966
approached. That condition is the subject of the
eighth poem of the series, "Season of Omens."

The extremity of political corruption, like the
violence that it inspired, is hard to convey in brief.
Clark begins with the violence, "When calabashes held
petrol and men turned faggots in the streets." Houses
and cars--"mansions and limousines"--were burnt too,
and "hoodlums took possession of police barracks."
These hint at the horror of October 1965 to January
1966 in the Western Region of Nigeria. Some sample
headlines from the Daily Times (Lagos) confirm
Clark's words: "16 KILLED IN RIOTS AT IJEBU, OWO
AREAS" (November 9, 8-9); "MAN ROASTED TO DEATH IN REMO
AREA" (December 10, 2); on December 16, the entire
front page was devoted to an almost hysterical editorial comment, bannered "IT CANNOT GO ON. IT MUST NOT GO
ON" and "THIS MUST CEASE." The violence did not cease.
By mid-January, it had become impossible to leave the
city of Lagos by automobile because thugs controlled
the roads.

What had started as political violence had taken on
a quality and direction of its own. Hoodlums, originally hired by politicians to intimidate the opposition,
had transcended intimidation to murder, arson, and
looting. Murder itself began as political action, and
as such it continued and accelerated with political
success and failure. Eventually it became, joined with
robbery, an objective in itself. Disorder became
horror.

One source of the disorder was the complex census of
1962-63 and 1963-64. Where power would lie in Nigeria
depended on population. The vast Northern Region contained more than half the population; as a result, the
dominant party was assured at least a plurality in the
Federal Parliament. Politicians in the North feared

that, if the three southern regions (plus Lagos) should
exceed the North in population, a southern alliance
could freeze them permanently out of power. The census
conducted on May 13, 1962, had exactly the feared
result. It was not a result to be trusted. As early
as May 1 the "discovery" had been revealed of a large
village in the East--20,000 people!--"which has neither
been registered for parliamentary elections, nor represented in any of the Nigerian legislatures" (3). This
was the first of the "clans" that Clark says "were
discovered that were not in the book." Clark then
alludes to the second census (the first was declared
void), in which the North, famous for production of
livestock, found an additional 7.3 million people,
restoring its population majority. Clark has it, "cattle [were] counted for the heads of men." The metaphor
is apt: an observer reported that one junior Northern
official was counted six times (4).

The census was the basis for elections, and the quarrel over the census wrecked an already unsteady alliance between the party dominant in the North and the
dominant Eastern party. In turn, the federal election
of December 30, 1964, was so bitterly fought that
Nigeria verged on chaos. Over the New Year, the President of the nation refused to acknowledge the result.
It was undeniably corrupt and it retained in power
those already in power. He delayed until January 6
reappointing the Prime Minister. He had by that date
formal assurance that the new government would be
"broadly based" (5). Essentially, and to widespread
disgust, the Prime Minister reappointed the old government, enlarging it with members from the North's new
allies in the West. This is Clark's "cabinet . . . so
broad the top gave way and trapped everyone therein."

The collapse of the government took just a year.
During that year a regional election in the West took
place. This was the election that institutionalized
murder, arson, and looting. In the process "hoodlums
took possession of police barracks" and "women grew
heavy with ballot papers," Clark says correctly and
literally. Some thugs were simply hired as police (6);
others overpowered the police. The police themselves
were responsible for women having possession of large
numbers of ballots. The Electoral Commission had entrusted the ballots to the Commissioner of Police;
hundreds upon hundreds were discovered in unauthorized

hands. A reporter for West Africa personally verified one of the many reports of women "pregnant" with paper (7).

"Season of Omens" also mentions money "kept in infant's skulls with full blessing of prelates" and "men" who "lost their teeth before they could cut them to eat corn." These lines are perhaps more suggestive than literal, though it is quite clear that vast sums in bribe money were hidden at home because bank deposits could be investigated with compromising results, and it is also in the record that no less a prelate than the Roman Catholic Archbishop of Lagos accepted valuable property from a corrupt official at a lease rental of one shilling per year. The property was said to be irrelevant to the priest's clerical duties (8).

Finally, the poem includes a reference to a great and immediate cause of indignation in early January 1966: "a grand vizier in season of arson turned upon bandits in a far off place." While the Western Region was (almost literally) on fire, the Prime Minister's major concern was Rhodesia, where Ian Smith had lately unilaterally declared independence. A Commonwealth Conference to deal with the remote problem convened at Lagos; it was the first such conference to be held outside of London. Distracting though it might be, the conference was irrelevant to the horror at home. Worse, as soon as the conference ended, the Prime Minister publicly announced that he would take no action at all in regard to the chaos in the West.

Though the Prime Minister would take no action, fear was widespread that since something had to be done, something surely would. Perhaps most likely was a ruthless crushing of the opposition in the West by a combination of police and army. What did happen was that a group of young majors revolted against the political leaders and senior army officers in an attempt to create a new political order.

The recurrent line following each line of outrage in "Season of Omens" is the contrasting folkloric line, "Then came the five hunters." After that litany, the poem changes to folk imagery:

> At club closure
> Antelopes slept, for lions snored;
> Then struck the five hunters . . .

Casualties 135

At this point, the poem shifts from omens to action, from causes for the January 15, 1966, coup to the coup itself.
   On that first night of action and blood many died. Who they were and why they died (and not others) must be understood to complete this account of the political situation and to prepare for the circumstances that motivated the entire series of poems. Clark writes:

> Fallen in the grass was the lion,
> Fallen in the forest was the jackal,
> Missing by the sea was the shepherd-sheep
> His castrate ram in tow,
> And all around was the blood of hounds.

   These symbolic animals recur. The "lion" is the Sardauna of Sokoto, Alhaji Sir Ahmadu Bello, the most powerful politician in Nigeria. His office as Premier of the Northern Region gave him leverage so that the Prime Minister was, when necessary, his agent, and all others had to deal with him or be locked out of authority. The "jackal" is Chief Samuel A. Akintola, Premier of the Western Region, who struck a deal with the Sardauna and thereby betrayed the party that had put him in power. It was his desperation to retain his office, and the desperation of his enemies to displace him that brought chaos and horror to the West. The "shepherd-sheep" and the "castrate ram" are the Prime Minister, Alhaji Sir Abubakar Tafawa Balewa, a gentle and honorable man who nevertheless fronted for the Sardauna, and Chief Festus Okotie-Eboh, the corrupt Federal Finance Minister who was as notorious for his fat and extravagance as for his corruption. The "hounds" are most of the ranking officers of the Nigerian Army; the largest number of the dead among them were, by coincidence or determination, popular and admired officers from the Northern Region--a fact to have great significance later on.
   The poem hints at the circumstances of the killings. The Sardauna fell "in the grass" of the north: he was at his house in the northern capital, Kaduna, which lies in the grass belt of sub-Sudanic Nigeria. Akintola fell "in the forest," at Ibadan, a great city in the forest belt of southern Nigeria. Tafawa Balewa and Okotie-Eboh were "missing by the sea"; they were

found days later, it was reported, near the Lagos-Abeokuta road. Lagos, where they had been seized, is the Nigerian capital and chief port. In each case soldiers--"hounds"--died, but the greatest mortality was at Lagos, with Kaduna second. No one was killed at Enugu, capital of the East, or Benin, capital of the Mid-West. Virtually all of the "five hunters" were from those two regions--most, indeed, from the East.

With the action of "the five hunters" the political situation was dramatically transformed. How it happened and what the results were will be dealt with later. Now it is necessary to consider one of the "hunters" in particular and Clark's relationship to him and to a mutual friend; both are significant to these poems.

The "five hunters" may for present purposes be treated as symbolic of the four to seven officers (six majors, apparently, and a captain) who originated the plan. They are as well symbolic of the whole cadre of fourteen or more officers who carried it out. For Clark, the chief was his friend Major Emmanuel A. Ifeajuna, the "Emman" of "Skulls and Cups." He is the "Leader of the Hunt," the tenth poem, and he is the principal speaker in the eleventh, "Conversation at Accra." He and his association with Clark and Christopher Okigbo--also a skull in "Skulls and Cups"--must be understood.

Okigbo is, in a way, the key character. Although he was graduated from University College, Ibadan, in 1956, he remained near UCI the next few years while Clark and Ifeajuna were students. Then he spent a year as librarian and teacher at the University of Nigeria, Nsukka, in the East, returning to Ibadan to work for Oxford University Press (9). At Ibadan Okigbo encouraged Clark to publish his poetry, and they became close friends. Ifeajuna was best known at Ibadan as an athlete; he won the gold medal for the high jump at the Commonwealth Games (10). To Clark he was a contemporary, active in the Student Union, and his origins were eastern, like Okigbo's. With both it seems he shared political sympathies. It has been said of Ifeajuna that from his university days he "had wide contacts with radical intellectuals in the civil service and universities" (11). Martin J. Dent has suggested that the Ibadan intellectuals in 1965 were characterized by an "unfortunate longing for bloodshed" and that there existed a "sort of milieu of violent thought in some radical Ibadan circles." He specifies that Ifeajuna came to the army from this Ibadan environment (12). Okigbo and Clark were part of that environment, although Clark in the mid-1960s lived in Lagos.

Okigbo welcomed the coup. In December of 1965, a month before the coup, at Ibadan, he wrote, "The smell of blood already floats in the lavender-mist of the afternoon. / The death sentence lies in ambush along the corridors of power / . . ." Clark, as editor of Black Orpheus, published the poem in 1968 (with note of the place and date) (13). After the coup, in "Hurrah for Thunder," dated January 17, 1966, Okigbo announced, "the elephant has fallen-- / Hurrah for Thunder--" clearly celebrating the death of the Sardauna. Thus Okigbo, wholly ignorant of details about the plot, anticipated it and hoped for its success. It is evident that Clark did too.

The interconnection of Ifeajuna, Okigbo, and Clark is central to the poems. Clark has said, in his "Preface to Notes" in Casualties, "I got so close to a number of the actors after the curtain rose [on the crisis] . . . that I came to be identified by some as playing in the show" (Casualties, 54). It is possible to accept this disclaimer without doubting that Clark was a highly interested observer of the action. In the nineteenth poem, "The Flood," Clark expresses his relationship to the others:

> I flounder in my nest, a kingfisher,
> Whose flockmates would play
> At eagles and hawks, but like
> Chickens are swept away.

The kingfisher's flockmates--Ifeajuna and perhaps Okigbo as well as others--have set in motion a chain of events they, seen through Clark's isolated and confused perspective, seemed too weak or inept to control. Clark, friend and observer, shares in the effects that they have set in motion.

What did the rebellious majors, "the five hunters," do? A description of their plan and its outcome is essential background to the poems. Dan Izevbaye has said of Clark's note on "The Leader of the Hunt," "Here, as elsewhere in the book, the accompanying notes provide more information than is necessary for an under-

standing of the poems" (14). His statement was no
doubt true of himself when he wrote it, but others,
more distant in time or place from the events, lack the
immediate experience of having lived through the days.
For the new reader today allusions to events well known
at the time are not enough. The critic needs as well
at least some of the facts, presented as Clark seems to
have expected them to be understood.

Insofar as a scenario for the rebels can be reconstructed, it appears something like the following.
Their first objectives were to clear out two groups
that would block their assumption of power. The first
was the major political figures. These included the
federal Prime Minister and the four regional premiers.
The second group was those ranking officers of the army
who were unlikely to support the rebels' radical program. After clearing the way to power, the rebels
would institute a strong central administration for the
nation while fragmenting the powerful regions. Then it
seems they planned to invite a civilian leader they
respected to govern. The removal, by arrest or assassination, of all the crucial political and military
figures was to be accomplished in a night. A central
problem was that the people to be removed were scattered among the various capitals. Thus the plan required that action begin where the best opportunities
were, and then be completed swiftly enough to prevent
effective reaction.

Lagos and Kaduna, on January 15, 1966, were the
appropriate places to start. Major C. K. Nzeogwu and
Major T. Onwuatuegwu and others were to kill the
Sardauna and two senior officers, Brigadier S. A.
Ademulegun and Colonel R. A. Shodeinde. They were also
to arrest politicians, control the area, and win the
support of the remaining officers. Then they were to
secure Zaria and Kano, through Major F. E. Akagha (who
would kill his superior--though this proved unnecessary) at Zaria and Lt. Colonel O. Ojukwu at Kano, if he
would cooperate. This part of the plan went off
perfectly--or seemed to, at first.

In the sixth poem, "The Cockerel in the Tale," Clark
details the action as an animal tale. The "lion"
Sardauna was killed and his "den," his house, rich in
art and treasures, destroyed. The "rogue elephant"
Ademulegun and "his brood," his wife, were both killed.
The "bull" Shodeinde was killed too, possibly "shot in

the eye" as Clark describes. Then, having acted, Nzeogwu could only await results in the South. Aside from proclamations and television interviews, he could do little more. As Clark says, he "proclaimed / The break of day" although he was "uncertain then / Where the sun would rise."

In Lagos the plan was more complex. Most of the army officers scheduled for elimination were in Lagos, as was the prime minister. But the premier of the West was in Ibadan, over a hundred miles by road to the north. Worse, the premiers of the Mid-West and East were much farther away so surprises at Benin and Enugu could really not be hoped for. Indeed, action in those capitals may have been ruled out from the start: the military units were not significant, and the Eastern premier had, in his house as a guest, a Commonwealth head of state.

What actually happened, in summary, is this. Ifeajuna with two lieutenants (newly brought into the plan) and twenty-two other-rank soldiers arrested the prime minister and, possibly on impulse, arrested also the minister of finance, who lived nearby. Major C. I. Anuforo, with a lieutenant and six soldiers, went to the homes of Colonel Kuru Mohammed and Lt. Colonel A. Unegbe. Both were shot. Later Anuforo killed Lt. Colonel J. Y. Pam, who had been arrested by others. Major D. O. Okafor had responsibility for killing Brigadier Zak Maimalari, but he escaped. Maimalari, seeking refuge, saw in a car Ifeajuna, his brigade major, and called to him to stop. Ifeajuna killed him. Ifeajuna then killed Lt. Colonel A. Largema in the hall of the Ikoyi Hotel.

Another conspirator, Captain E. N. Nwobosi, meanwhile had taken a detachment of soldiers from Abeokuta, where he and they were stationed, to Ibadan. There they killed Akintola, the premier of the West. Nwobosi was an almost last-minute recruit to the plan; though successful, he was in the strict sense not one of the "five hunters." And he was not able to secure control of his own garrison (as Nzeogwu had successfully done in Kaduna).

Ifeajuna and Okafor also failed in the crucial act of securing military control. The General Officer Commanding the Army, Major General J. T. U. Aguiyi-Ironsi, was in Lagos and by luck or by error escaped assassination. Ironsi took command of police headquarters and

then the military forces at Ikeja. Lt. Colonel Yakubu
Gowon, also safe, helped rally troops into the command
structure. Ojukwu at Kano (who apparently did not know
of the coup in advance) gave the rebels no support.
Ifeajuna, when he and Okafor learned of Ironsi's beginning to take control, drove with the prime minister out
of Lagos on the Abeokuta road, stopped, and shot him,
leaving the body. They then proceeded on a nearly ten-
hour drive to Enugu, a drive that took them through
Benin. Neither the premier in Benin nor the premier in
Enugu was killed. Ifeajuna did talk with the Eastern
premier, Dr. M. I. Okpara, before going into hiding
(eventually reaching Ghana) (15).

This is the story behind "The Leader of the Hunt"
(which is not, as Ezekiel Mphahlele imagined, about
Ojukwu, nor is the "god about to fall" President
Houphuet-Boigny of the Ivory Coast, as Mphahlele hoped
[16]). Unexplained in the poem are things too personal
for history (for example, the "love or kiss / Of housewife or harlot" from which the leader grew mad), but
"Helped over stile by several hands with key / To
surgery or bedroom, decked at one point / As a belle
. . ." is clear enough: Okigbo provided Ifeajuna with
an elaborate escape route to Ghana (17). Clear too is
the "trail / Of brass all loaded with lead."

The dead "brass" raise the question Clark seems to
ask in "Conversation at Accra." Returning to the image
of the hunt and dogs, he asks Ifeajuna "Why in the hunt
did the pack / Fall on its own kind?" The hunter
replies, "Because the hounds at the head of the pack
played with the lion / . . . hunted for the lion," in
clear reference to the Sardauna and his close personal
friend Brigadier Ademulegun, as well as other officers
loyal to the "lion." The poem alludes to yet others:
"One in fact gave fangs to the hyrax, / Called into the
kennel the jackal." This points to Brigadier Maimalari, who on May 25, 1962, watched as supporters of
Premier Akintola ("the jackal") rioted in the Western
House of Assembly, deliberately provoking a fraudulent
"State of Emergency" by which democratic process under
the constitution came to an end; Maimalari was, in
fact, in command of the armed forces in the West at
that time (18). The hyrax would seem to be Dr.
Okpara, the Eastern premier, who in 1962 supported
Akintola (he changed his support after the census
conflict). The poem goes on to identify Lt. Colonel

Pam, an officer of Tiv origins who commanded troops sent to restore order during the Tiv riots of 1964 (19): "Another was sent / As plague upon his breed."

In something like a dramatic aside, Ifeajuna half-absolves the guilty politicians and soldiers by putting blame on "the keeper," the British. They, he says, created the situation his murders were designed to resolve:

> Oh, rabid
> The day the keeper delivered
> All in the grassland to the lion,
> All in the forest to the leopard.

The "grassland to the lion" is clear enough (the North to the Sardauna) but "the forest to the leopard" is less clear. Clark's <u>leopard</u> is a variable symbol. Here it seems to mean the politicians of the South--West as well as East--though it could mean the politicians of the East alone since Nigeria's first government when the British withdrew was an alliance of the North and East, an alliance from which the West was largely excluded. The leopard at any rate is unpredictable, in life, as in these poems.

The poem concludes with a recapitulation of the revolutionary program: a new nation, reconstituted, divided into smaller states so none could dominate, with at its head the imprisoned political leader Chief Obafemi Awolowo, whose resistance to Akintola precipitated the 1962 crisis and led to the 1965 chaos in the West.

> I sought to build
> A new estate of fourteen wings,
> Each interlocked with the other
> Around an open court.
> I sought to post by each gate
> A watchdog, summon to service
> Hands that never held dirt,
> And upon the stool in the hall
> I thought to sit a man,
> Burnt clean by fires he had
> Himself started.

But "Overnight" the plan has failed and "straws / In the wind spell no design."

Identification of the poem with a specific political program may obscure a strength of the poem. Clark's metaphor of the "estate," with the gates and watchdogs and an enstooled Chief, is effective in itself in an imaged poetic world. Throughout this discussion the reader should keep in mind that the underlying real events and programs are only a context for the poems, never a substitute.

The unwelcome, unsought outcome of the coup was the installation of Ironsi as head of government, suggested in the fifth poem, "The Usurpation." The politicians were helpless. Against the military, a state with no constitutional government (the acting president refused to appoint an acting prime minister) had no order of command. The British high commissioner met with politicians ("envoys, alien and local") and the inconclusive outcome was that the nation had no head. Ironsi was given command.

Clark implies that from the start Ironsi had little idea of how to proceed. To deal with Ifeajuna, he sent Okigbo to Ghana with promises of a good reception upon Ifeajuna's "Return Home," recorded in the poem of that title. There was to have been "the red rug" and a "horse"; instead a "donkey" carried the major off to detention. Ironsi may have wished to honor the rebels, but did not dare do so. In the end, he died before he made up his mind how finally to treat them. His treatment of Ifeajuna was a reflection, in a way, of the major's reception in Ghana. Kwame Nkrumah, Ghana's head of state (who was about to be deposed in a coup), at first honored Ifeajuna, then jailed him, as indicated in "The Leader of the Hunt." He had been embarrassed by having responsibility for the rebel thrust upon him, and by the resultant implication that Ghana had inspired and supported the coup. Okigbo and the Nigerian high commissioner only with difficulty secured Ifeajuna's release.

Ironsi had many problems. The conspirators' uncertain fate was a major one. It interlinked with another severe problem: he tried to conceal the nature and dimension of the killings. This is the subject of Clark's sixth poem, "The Burden in Boxes." The conspirators had been mostly Igbo in origin (that is, from the dominant Eastern language group); the dead were overwhelmingly Northern. Since Ironsi too was Igbo, it was inevitable that a false belief should arise in a

continuing "Igbo Plot." That belief was exacerbated by
Ironsi's "folly," as Martin Dent has described it:

> The death of the army officers was never published; there was no funeral service, an important element in the military mind, without which the injury done to the dead was made twice as great; there was no public eulogy. It was as though these officers had never existed. . . . Among the private soldiers the rumours kept spreading that Maimalari was alive and coming to rally them. To many of the Northern soldiers he was a kind of hero-figure. (20)

The once-heroic conspirators gradually came to be seen by Northern soldiers as sinister collaborators in an Igbo design to rule Nigeria permanently, while the fellow-soldier victims became incitements to revenge.

Ironsi, whom Clark symbolizes through his stuffed crocodile walking stick, ruled until the end of July. His "acolytes" in the seventh poem, "The Reign of the Crocodile," were his own friends. Ironsi was already long known for selection of aides "for congeniality and ability to out-drink him" (21). But the final lines, describing his six-month rule,

> He sat down to a party,
> Called in his cronies, and
> Not one knew the song,

surely allude, though unjustly, to the Igbo intellectuals who became his dominant advisors. These included, very prominently, "Chris's" brother, Dr. Pius Okigbo, a distinguished economist. Most prominent was Francis Nwokedi. To Nwokedi Ironsi gave the task of programming the unification of public services (22). The result was abolition of the regional federation on May 24. Nwokedi's program was an excellent one, but its timing proved a fatal error. The decree almost instantly provoked murderous attacks upon Igbos in the North. Clark's thirteenth poem, "The Locust Hunt," expresses the horror of that sudden revenge, so greatly in excess of its provocation. The decree provoked the killings because it seemed final proof that the whole January action was an orchestrated exercise in Igbo domination. "What the Squirrel Said" is Clark's account of the rumors and their effect--the squirrel, he says in his note, is oracle to the python (<u>Casualties</u>, 57); the python is the rage that concludes the poem. After recalling the killing of one animal in the poem, the squirrel remembers another equally (or similarly) vicious animal left alive. The lion killed, but not the leopard, the bull but not the boar, the elephant but not the crocodile, the sheep but not the hyrax. The dead correspond to the animals in "The Cockerel in the Tale" and "Season of Omens," and the crocodile and hyrax remain Ironsi and Okpara. The leopard appears to suggest the East in Ojukwu, the senior Igbo officer after Ironsi and Military Governor in the East. The boar possibly represents the other unmurdered Premier, Chief Dennis Osadebay of the Mid-West. The dead in this poem are all men of the North, while the survivors are all of the East (or allied, as was Osadebay).

The squirrel's word, and the crocodile's folly, led at last to the counter coup of July 29. In it not only was Ironsi killed but for a time soldiers (and others) from the East were slaughtered by Northern soldiers who rebelled in many cases against their own officers. It was a literally terrible week, with "leopards [here the soldier-murderers generally] amok from the forest," as Clark says in the fourteenth poem, "July Wake." The "cat in a mouse hide" whose final hours are described in that poem surely is Ironsi, although the fairly precise account in the poem does not as precisely match any other source. Generally, however, the poem, which tells of the "four hours" while the cat waited, "uncheered by faces / Over hedge, voices over telephone, / And even the 999 [police telephone emergency number] squad / He called in," generally agrees with this account:

> Though surrounded by the mutineers and his own guard disarmed, Ironsi was, curiously, still able to contact people by telephone. He called Gowon and asked him to send a helicopter. Police headquarters in Lagos sent one, but by the time it had arrived the general had disappeared. A senior police officer in Ibadan . . . was told to keep away . . . by the commander of the local garrison. (23)

Eventually Ironsi and his host, "the gallant Military Governor of Western Nigeria, Lt. Col. Adekunle Fajuyi"

(Casualties, 58), were arrested, beaten, and taken away in police vans to be shot and buried. Clark has a "gang in green" fling Ironsi beaten and "passed mercifully / By now beyond dispatch" into the "boot" of a car. (Now, the poem concludes, the passing of a "car . . . hooting by" evokes "the roar / Of leopards amok in the forest.")

The awful time that followed, during which Clark, Okigbo, and a multitude of others fled to their homes, is further defined in the fifteenth, sixteenth, and seventeenth poems, "Exodus," "August Afternoon," and "The Rat in the Hole." In the last Clark writes,

> Cooped in my hole,
> I cringe as a rat
> Upon a rising mound
> Of fear

while from the East "the sun" calls "all to thunder." In the confusion that followed the July coup, two Nigerias had come into being and civil was was certain (though the quest for peace delayed the battle until nearly a year later). The second Nigeria was the Eastern Region, where the counter coup had failed, and Ojukwu ("the sun"? a rising sun became a symbol for the East when he declared it independent Biafra) defied the new government in Lagos, headed by Gowon.

The same three poems reflect real and profound fears that Gowon was an instigator and supporter of the July and August murders, that Nigeria at last was ruled by Northerners who would never again allow power to escape their hands, that the new rulers would hunt down to kill all who were in any way associated with Ironsi's government. As Clark puts it in "August Afternoon," "a column of rats / Scales over roofs / After cats."

Incidents continued occasionally in August. Gowon temporized, clearly uncertain as to the best future course. For a time the most likely outcome seemed to be "confederation" (Daily Times, August 25), with each region autonomous. Clark, in his note to "July Wake," calls this "partition" (Casualties, 59). In early September it appeared that the North, the West, and the East were prepared to accept confederation, though it meant effective dissolution of the nation. Clark's note indirectly explains why his own region, the Mid-West, rejected the apparently popular solution.

As the note is not repeated in the 1981 text Decade of Tongues, it is appropriate to reproduce the second paragraph from Casualties here in full:

> Once home, I discovered that partition of the country would not stop at the boundaries of region nor of tribe, but would go to the last unit of clan and of village as obtained in large areas of the country before the British came. And so too would be the division of assets and liabilities. For example, the oil that flowed under much of the dispute and sparked it off into the open flames of secession and war, by the very logic of derivation, should revert not just to one region which, like the rest of the country, was an artificial creation and conglomeration of different and disparate peoples, but to the villages and clans out of whose soil the foreign companies are tapping it for their own gain. And even before the regions came, the country had been. Therefore, after a brief period of shock and doubt I returned in September to Lagos firm in my belief in a federal Nigeria in need of re-structuring and reform. (Casualties, 59)

Clark's position was a reflection of proposals that were made to an ad hoc Constitutional Conference that convened in Lagos September 12. By that time, the Western attitude had shifted and its proposals favored more states and a strong central government. Clark's Mid-West delegation favored even more states but with a somewhat weaker center. By mid-September only the Eastern delegates rejected a multi-state form with a central government that would be stronger than the pre-coup federation had been. Perhaps in the months to come a plan acceptable to all could have been worked out. Gowon, though a Northerner, was from a minority ethnic community and could be seen by other minority leaders as a leader of a coalition of minorities that would balance out the old Hausa-Yoruba-Igbo domination of Nigerian political life. Very likely this was Clark's view when he returned to Lagos in September.

But the constitutional conference had scarcely adjourned after its five-day first session when the greatest horror yet began. Soldiers joined with thugs in a decisive effort to eliminate all Igbos in the North. The eighteenth poem, "Dirge," reflects Clark's anguish in the escalating violence--six to ten thousand Igbo murdered (24) in alleged response to some rumored, and perhaps some real, killings and menacings of Northerners in the East (25):

> O let us light the funeral pile
> But let us not become its faggots

he cries.

This poem precedes "The Flood," which, it was said earlier, reflects Clark's relationship to his friends, whose loss is at the center of <u>Casualties</u>. It is a poem of disillusion, of failure, of lost hopes. It is the pivot upon which <u>Casualties</u> turns, reflecting on past hopes and failures, recognizing present (in the historical sense) incapacity, and anticipating the futility of seeking to avoid the disaster to come. The present time in the poem is near the end of that terrible year 1966. "The rain of events pours down," it begins, suggesting the mindlessness that seemed to govern political change (and introducing, not for the first time, the water imagery so marked in Clark's poetry). Against this rain, Clark--"Like a million other parakeets"--puts on a brilliant coat, "the finest silver and / Song can acquire." When that coat does not suffice, "I unfurl my umbrella, resplendent as any / That covers a chief / At a durbar," alluding to the great shows of horsemanship performed for emirs and governors on great occasions in the North. These lines, to Kolawole Ogungbesan, are "narcissistic indulgence in the midst of a national disaster" (26), but the judgment seems invalidated by the ironic tone-- almost self-satire--and by the lines that follow (which Ogungbesan does not quote): "It [the umbrella] buckles, and will / Fly out of my hand."

The point is that art (surely that is the meaning of "coat" and "umbrella" here) has no role in the events now tormenting Nigerians; instead there are "the grief / Gusts of rain," that nothing can protect one from, continuing relentlessly. The anguish here is almost hidden; the punning of "grief" disguises its meaning but makes it more poignant. The reader recognizes that Clark is identifying with his friends, Ifeajuna and Okigbo especially, in lines partly quoted earlier,

> I flounder in my nest, a kingfisher,

>   Whose flockmates would play
>   At eagles and hawks, but like
>   Chickens, are swept away
>   By flood fed from septic tanks, till
>   Together, we drift and drown,
>   Who were at home on sea, air, and land. (27)

They are, he says, together, filthily caught in the flood of events, deprived now of their common freedom of art and imagination. To the reader who was perhaps a participant in the events, Clark's metaphor of "flockmates" who "play / At eagles and hawks" may be offensive. Surely Ifeajuna, Okigbo, and the others did not "play" at killing and being killed. In context, however, in the ironic distancing and understatement that marks these poems, the tone is appropriate. Clark, who dares "not look at" friends in "Song," does not look at them in "The Flood." Instead all "drift and drown," a painful litotes for uncertainty and death.

To this point in <u>Casualties</u>, the poems have proceeded in two stages. First, the opening poems in which the time was after the events, the poet looking back. Second, an extended series of responses to increasingly dangerous and terrible circumstances. The poems have come now to a moment in which the only way in which those "friends . . . I have held in my arms" ("Song") are together is in helplessness and grief. From this point in <u>Casualties</u> the poems show an acceptance of circumstances, however terrible, beyond the poet's control. The war comes inevitably. Okigbo dies, as do Ifeajuna and other "faces / I dare not look at" ("Night Song"). Clark and others living remain. All, like Nigeria herself, are transformed.

The next poem after "The Flood" is a prologue to the war, set like "Skull and Cups" in time after the event. "Aburi and After" recalls the momentary optimism that greeted the gathering together of Gowon and the Military Governors, including Ojukwu of the East, in Ghana. It was early in the new year, January 4 and 5, 1967. Clark alludes to the unexpected cordiality among the soldiers ("They were wringing Jack Gowon's hand") and to the need to reconstruct a divided government ("a rule / Too broken then in the sand / To flog a fly"). These are countered by the bad faith (as Clark sees it) of both sides ("the scowl / Of implacable masks in the compound"). Gowon ("a keeper now at attention") stands for mediation and the hope of reconciliation. He is not undamaged ("ankle twisted"), for he violated the terms he agreed to at Aburi, but he has "A prayer in his heart" (28).

The failure of Aburi led to the civil war. The war is a new activity of the creature Clark in the next poem calls "The Beast." He says that

> the dragon by five young daemons
> Released out of their mad love of the land,
> Belches, gorged already with the feast
> That creates room as it fills the guts.

Killing is, he says, the provocation of killing,

> And blood calcifies into boulders
> For brother to hurl against brother.

In the opening days of the war, one of the first "brothers" to die was Christopher Okigbo.

Poem XXII, "Death of a Weaverbird," has been mistaken for "a song of direct lamentation over the death of a fellow poet" (29). It is not a lament. There is praise in the poem (though it is ambiguous):

> Clear was his voice as the siren's
> Chirp with no fixed hour
> Of ditty or discourse

but no "lamentation" at all. It begins rather coldly, distantly:

> Shot,
> At Akwebe,
> A place not even on the map
> Made available by Shell-BP,
> A weaverbird,

and it continues with recognition of Okigbo's lack of tribal feeling; it is an essentially political observation: his "inverted house / Had a straw from every soil" (30).

The point of the poem is contained in the final two lines, which are "A note / With a bullet for another:"

> How can I return to sing another song?

> To help start a counter surge?

The first of these lines at least partly implies "No more opportunity for the poet to continue creating" as the critic quoted earlier, Romanus Egudu, has said, but he is mistaken in thinking the final line refers to the opportunity of "the soldier to resume his fight." There is no resumption in a "counter surge" just as there is no repetition in "another song." To Clark, as was hinted early in this chapter, it must have seemed that, had he lived, Okigbo would surely have joined Ifeajuna and others in their resistance to the East's leadership in the war--and perhaps been executed like them for doing so.

The tragedy of <u>Casualties</u>, its poignancy even, lies not in the fact of death but in the chill isolation that death makes permanent. It is not the living whom Clark dare not look at, but the dead. The dead are those with whom Clark shared "bath and bed . . . dish . . . tea . . . wine," with whom

> When but to think of an ill, made
> By God or man, was to find
> The cure prophet and physician
> Did not have.
>
> ("Song")

Clark in "Death of a Weaverbird" rejects the possibility that what he shared with Okigbo would die with him, and (rightly or wrongly) insists that their common ground precluded their being enemies. That Okigbo had "no fixed hour / Of ditty or discourse" (his passion and unpredictability were among his most notable personal characteristics) led him to go blindly to his death; had he lived, could Ifeajuna and Sam Agbam have failed to enlist him in their plan to deal with Lagos (31)? Clark here, as in "Skulls and Cups," implicitly links "Chris" with "Emman" and "Sam." And, of course, with Clark himself. The isolation of death is not to be loss of all connection.

This is reinforced in "Friends." Clark says that the loss of friends is a shallow burden compared to "The loss to kin" because "Our loss, large as the fellowship / We kept" is by the largeness of that fellowship ("by that number") lessened. In "fellowship" then is the cushion against "loss." This in turn leads to

Casualties

the poem which deals with the diminishing of fellowship among those still living. It is "The Casualties" subheaded "To Chinua Achebe," the twenty-seventh poem.

"The Casualties," which begins, "The casualties are not only those who are dead," is prepared for in three poems about the war, "XXIV A Photograph in The Observer," "XXV Benin Sacrifice," and "XXVI Party Song." The first refers to a remarkable picture taken by Romano Cagnoni, captioned (in John de St. Jorre's The Brother's War) "Young men going to war; Biafran recruits, stripped to the waist and their heads shaved, arrive in a training camp" (32). The effect is endless twins ("ibeji," Yoruba twin figures, is Clark's image) prepared "for hurling at the ogre"--Gowon--"They all see in the dark." They are being prepared as weapons that may well die. Actually dying in "Benin Sacrifice" are two officers ("two rams . . . led / Hooded to stakes") to be shot for murder of civilians, just as in 1897 the British executed nobles of Benin for an ambush of British soldiers (33). In "Party Song" there is an ironic juxtaposition of "Brigades and Villages." Both are "going out / Like lights over Lagos." In something like the ordinary sense, these three poems reflect casualties of war.

Clark in "The Casualties" however enlarges the scope of the concept, beyond the dead and wounded, to include "those who have lost / Persons or property" and "those led away by night." Even "those who started / A fire and cannot now put it out," and the Eastern refugees collectively, "those who escaping / The shattered shell became prisoners in / A fortress of falling walls," are casualties. But the poet tells novelist Achebe (who traveled internationally in support of the separatist government), those are not the only casualties. Alluding apparently to Achebe himself, Clark says some are "the emissaries of rift," "the wandering minstrels" who draw an uncomprehending "world / Into a dance with rites it does not know."

Besides these, and at the heart of the poem, the poet, Achebe, and the rest, collectively,

> We fall,
> All casualties of the war,
> Because we cannot hear each other speak
> Because eyes have ceased to see the face from
>   the crowd,

because "We are characters now other than before / The war began." The condition of war becomes universal in the fragmentation of family, fellowship, and understanding, even of the self. Society (corrupt before, as in "Seasons of Omens") is corrupted anew, as it were, by "the looters for office / And wares, fearful every day the owners may return." These owners are those displaced (to, or from, the East, or North, or West) by war. The living are corrupted in their relations with each other; Clark and Achebe would, it seemed when the poem was written, surely never be reconciled.

> We are all casualties,
> All sagging as are
> The cases celebrated for kwashiorkor,
> The unforeseen camp-follower of not just our war.

"We are all," in a final grotesque image, "sagging" like those children described by Achebe,

> With washed-out ribs and dried-up
> bottoms struggling in laboured
> steps behind blown empty bellies . . . (34)

dying children, being killed by their starving bodies feeding upon themselves.

The "we" of the poem suffer a spiritual kwashiorkor, a transformation bordering on spiritual death in the isolation that the shattering of personal relationships has brought about. To Clark, the loss of the dead Okigbo and Ifeajuna is paralleled by the loss of other friends, less close perhaps (like Achebe) but still part of the "fellowship" that was love's cushion against grief in "Friends."

The final poem mingles friends lost with yet other victims of the war in a return to the theme that began Casualties, the faces Clark "dare not look at / Though I have sat it out in the sun." Night Song" recalls "strange and young" men, "Nyananyo, Amangala, / Boro," whose images conflict with "faces I loved," who died, too. Clark did not know them, but in the time that frames these poems it seems that those who died later must obscure those who died first.

Still it is Ifeajuna and Okigbo who resonate, in the second stanza of the poem. Each is recalled for the manner of his dying and the political circumstance of his death: Ifeajuna, "Trapped in a cell when the crocodile" fell, was later released for "his return to day" but was executed--"fell into a pit." Okigbo was one of

> Others, touched on
> A chord resonant to the root,
> Followed, at the great crossroads,
> A dance into the forest. Oh,
> How can woods echo a song
> That filled city halls?
> How can cantors of the song
> Abandon the service on the floor?

Finally, the poem recapitulates the beginning, when Ifeajuna's "song should have begun / A festival of three hundred tribes" (an implied contrast to the only three "tribes" that dominated in precoup Nigeria), but "Instead . . . lit for Cantor / And chorus a funeral pile." This leads to the present time of the composition of the poem, when Gowon, once "Ignored by all as dumb," now "Catches the strain." He, Clark says, can provide for Nigeria, and for the secessionists,

> the house,
> Of our dream, with a mansion
> For them who followed ghosts
> Into the forests of night.

This recapitulation and, especially, this optimism are not so poetically effective as the ending to Casualties should be, but the defect is not fatal.

Casualties, experienced with understanding and acceptance of its context, is remarkably evocative. The transformation of mad politics into "Season of Omens" and of Ironsi's tragic failure into "The Reign of the Crocodile," and the massive energy of war in "The Beast" are among the fine poems dealing with public events. Coupled with their vigor and clarity are the more personal poems that, beginning coldly in "Skulls and Cups," detail the harsh progress from hope to anguish in separation and loss: "Leader of the Hunt," "Conversation at Accra," "The Flood," "Death of a Weaverbird," "Friends," "The Casualties." There is no lament in these poems. The controlling image is the poet's look at the sun. The tone is ironic and bitter. The pain is extreme, but it is not sorrow.

Clark is, as it were, the protagonist in his own poetic drama; his antagonist is the flood (always his favorite image), beyond the control of man, poet, or state. The flood washes out friendship, fellowship, friends themselves, and art is useless, coming late only to look upon the debris. If a hope is less than perfectly attached to the end, it is the poet's human failing. Clark has not disguised his failing. Rather it is part of all that these poems are about.

"Epilogue to Casualties"

In Decade of Tongues (1981) Clark added a twenty-ninth poem to Casualties, "Epilogue . . . To Michael Echeruo" (Decade, 88-89). This new poem makes a much more satisfying conclusion to the series than the final lines of "Night Song," for, while it affirms the point of view of the earlier poem, it is distanced from the time and emotion. It was written several years after the 1967-70 war ended, and (properly speaking) should not fit into Decade of Tongues, which is subtitled Selected Poems: 1958-1968. It is nevertheless welcome.

It is directed to Michael J. C. Echeruo, who had been part of the Ibadan group active in the Student Union when Clark and Ifeajuna were active also. Clark and Echeruo both matriculated at University College, Ibadan, in 1955, two of only 133 students admitted that year. They shared the pre-Independence experiences of resistance to school authorities in the "Communist scare" of the late 1950s, the supposedly hazardous visit of Queen Elizabeth to the campus, and a Student Union campaign for the removal of campus fences. Clark alludes to this last in a cryptic note about Ifeajuna perhaps "acting in character, running away after disrupting authority, as he had done while a student at Ibadan and Onitsha during the incidents of burglar-grille breaking and strike in both institutions" (Casualties, 57). The incident has a history.

At Ibadan, the president of the Student Union to his horror discovered a girl dead in his room, victim of an abortion attempt. He immediately called the police, but as a result of the ensuing scandal the university authorities undertook to fence off the student hostels in an apparent effort to prevent illicit sexual activity. The union demanded removal of the fences, and,

when the demand was refused, conspired to destroy them.
Echeruo himself was a conspirator, as were Clark and
Ifeajuna. On the night of the planned destruction, the
future rebel leader stayed in his room. Echeruo went
to his room to enlist his participation. Ifeajuna refused. But the fences were torn down that night, the
students were all sent away for a time, and the fences
were not replaced (35).

The story illustrates the commonality of experience
Echeruo shared with the important figures in Casualties. When the 1966 crisis reached its height,
Echeruo flead east with Okigbo and others, like the
novelist Chinua Achebe, to become active eventually in
the civil war on the secessionist side. After the war
Echeruo became head of the English department at the
University of Nigeria, Nsukka, in the East Central
State--the region that had been at the heart of the
resistance to federal rule. Later he was appointed to
a similar position at his alma mater, now the University of Ibadan. While there, he and Clark resumed their
friendship.

The poem, a reminiscence of a journey, tells of
Clark's revisiting places he knew because of friends
now dead "or gone now to their own homesteads." The
reconstruction of the war-shattered East Central State
was well advanced, yet ruins remained, "a vision of the
unnatural / Disaster that is war." The poem pauses
briefly at "Ogidi, strangely without / Pockmarks,
hamlet of the fabulist / Who I thought would never
forgive, never forget, / Knowing the wrong in his own
heart." The "fabulist" is Achebe, victim of Clark's
charge that he was one of "the emissaries of rift"
during the war.

The substantial pause in the poem is at Onitsha, the
Niger's great market city, but this comes only after a
jeer at Ojukwu and his comrades who flew to safety at
the end of the war, "swearing to fight to the last man
/ Even as they fled orphan, widow, and batman."

Onitsha is described in forceful images.

   Here houses, scalped and scarred past surgery,
   Stared at me, sightless in their sockets, like
   The relics of shell-shock that they are.
   One, so mutilated, it is a miracle
   The parts hung together at all,
   Called to me in the crush, in it one

    Plump woman, careless of her bare breast
    And brood, pounding yam up on a balcony,
    Tilted in the face of gravity.

In the second of those images, especially, Clark evokes the persistence of life in the ruins of war. From it he goes on to see the city "wreck" beside the river, "A widow who has also buried her seeds." At last, in a kind of resurrection, he says "The old market of dreams" rises. Beyond it rival cathedrals persist, "still in conflict / For eastern pastures, as they were before the war." The concluding irony is more convincing, more Clark's natural tone, than the sentimental "house / Of our dream" that marred the end of <u>Casualties</u> in "Night Song."

Incidental Songs

The <u>Casualties</u> section of the volume was linked to such passionate feelings at the time of publication that all attention seemed focused on those twenty-eight poems. If the others were read at all, there is little evidence in the critical literature. Yet they are not without interest.

"Incident at the Police Station, Warri" may even reflect back on <u>Casualties</u> in its portrayal of the cruel punishment of a naked prisoner before a "scared, curious throng" while "three very important / Looking persons" and "one gallant and another" nearby talk or proposition indifferently nearby. It is, Clark says, suggested by <u>The Flagellation of Jesus</u> by Piero della Francesca, and the comparison is accurate. It also recalls Auden's <u>Musée des Beaux Arts</u>, though Clark's is a far more violent poem.

"The Lagos-Ibadan Road before Shagamu" ironically observes an overloaded passenger lorry driven by a marijuana-intoxicated driver who escaped unhurt and is missing--while all fifty-odd passengers died. "A Lamp by my Window" is an image of a refracted moon. "To my Academic Friends who sit tight on their Doctoral Theses and have no Chair for Poet or Inventor" is a fine, cryptic poem, wholly spoiled by its explicit title.

There probably are political implications in "Nairobi National Park" and "Addis Ababa." The first is dedicated to the novelist-playwright James Ngugi, a critic of his government in Kenya. The lines, "Shy in the grass / The lion lies, / And placid are the ponds / In Embakasi Plain" may imply something more than a game park picture. Almost certainly the "dinosaur out / Of the Abyssinian lake" who leads the buffaloes in "Addis Ababa" is the aging Haile Selassie, and the poem is an invocation of his reactionary rule.

"A God is a Cow," "The Players," "Bombay," and "Calcutta," the concluding poems, are all poems of India. Clark's pen is characteristically venomous about England. England is "the old company / That made paupers of moguls" (though one may question Clark's accuracy), and is implied in the grime that "sits brandishing rags / In the wake of an empress now slut." Those lines are from "Bombay." "The Players" is more interesting, particularizing poverty in a street show:

> Thrilled today at the dazzle
> Of a rupee the girl can only touch
> On the way to a shallow till,
> The beggar boy moves scene
> For hag to play drum
> Majorette to her man . . .

Clark is more often at his best, as in this poem, when he depends least upon the purely verbal turn. Too much such dependence mars "Letter from Kampala," the least effective poem in the collection.

The incidental poems are Clark's most recent published poems (except for the "Epilogue to Casualties" of course). <u>Decade of Tongues</u> adds no others. This implies that for more than a decade Clark's lyric muse maintained a dignified silence. Perhaps it has been a silence in the face of the criticism, harsher than was deserved, that <u>Casualties</u> suffered.

Chapter Six
Prospects

In 1980 Clark retired as Professor of English at the University of Lagos. His reason for so early a retirement appears in a poem from his new collection of poems, State of the Union (not yet published):

Retirement

>That air and light may come again
>Clean and free into the chambers
>Of my heart, I give up, perhaps
>In folly, my tenure in a tower,
>Built upon a place of swamp.
>I had thought, standing in the cesspool,
>Head, shoulders and trunk above
>The stench, the rot around could not
>Infect my life. But feet in boots
>Over years of no reclamation
>Grew fetid, and lungs that were clear
>Before so much congested,
>It would have been suicide
>To stay any day longer,
>Believing one might as well accept
>The conditions, since they were
>After all endemic to the country.

The poem shows that Clark's bitter irony, his earthy imagery, and his political interest have not waned during his decade of silence as a lyric poet and dramatist. What is surprising is the lack of traditional imagery (a point which will be returned to shortly). The poem makes clear that Clark left academia gladly, and his remarkable productivity since his retirement strongly suggests that the air and light of his Kiagbodo home at Funama are indeed cleaner and freer than those of Lagos.

By April of 1981 State of the Union had been finished, and in that same month The Boat, the first play of a trilogy concerning Ngbilebiri history, was produced at Lagos and later performed on tour in Benin and Port Harcourt to enthusiastic audiences. Currently, Clark is writing a chronicle of a character in The Boat, Ambakederemo, Clark's great grandfather, who died in 1926 having lived through the great changes in Delta life during most of the preceding century. In short, Clark, in "retirement," seems to be at the start of a new period of productivity. The present moment, then, is an excellent one for review and projection.

Clark's poetry and drama have developed from the earliest themes of grief and loss, through paradox that accords with the simultaneous dangers and joys of life in the Delta, into celebration of the past (Ozidi) and the bitter irony of the present (Casualties). The poetry in particular has been occasional. Over the years, the poetry grew increasingly political, in direct proportion with its bitterness and irony. At the same time, the poetry drew increasingly on the kind of imagery that predominated in the drama: the imagery of traditional beliefs, tales, and life, especially those of the Ijo. In the drama, Clark began in a neoclassic mode, then shifted through modernism into the festive drama of the Ijo creeks. In his translation of the The Ozidi Saga, Clark brought to its climax an evolving idea of all his work: to re-create in the English language some substantial part of African spiritual reality, an essential aspect of the universal human reality.

Nevertheless, it would be an error to find any single controlling idea in Clark's work. His is an impulsive genius, surprising, sensitive, and reactive. The harsh treatment of the United States, in America, Their America, that offended so many people was no momentary aberration. Twenty-five years later, in State of the Union, Clark writes of Nigeria--his Nigeria--"Here Nothing Works":

> What is it in ourselves or in our soil
> That things which connect so well elsewhere,
> Like the telephone, the motorway, the airways,
> Dislocate our lives so much that we all
> Begin to doubt our own intelligence?

Clark is as responsive as ever. State of the Union demonstrates that he is no less critical of his own country than of others.

What has changed in Clark's poetry is the imagery. In State of the Union the semi-Europeanized nation is described literally, as in "The Plague,"

> Nobody now
> May go out any time of day
> For fear of gunmen ready
> To kill as be killed for a car

or in the title poem,

> It was never a union. It was at best
> An amalgamation, so said in fact
> The foreign adventurers who forged it.

In both poems, the central metaphors are in the titles. One poem in the group is an exception in being purely symbolic and imagistic--yet it too bears its ironic metaphor only in its title:

Progress

> The sandboats on the lagoon,
> Will they make the last mile
> Home by sunset? The wind,
> Stalling in their sails,
> Has travelled a thousand miles
> Since they set out at dawn.

The exceptional lines, and poems such as "Progress," prove the rule for Clark's latest poems: he has, for the time being at least, put aside his traditional motif for a clearer, more discursive verse.

That the change may be temporary--or indeed only occasional--is suggested by "Other Songs on Other States," which complete the new volume of poems. Most of these recall Clark's early poetry of grief and loss, but in a voice that is more mature. Several, including some of the best, are discursive and literal accounts of the deaths and funerals of friends or others beloved. But others are more imagistic and metaphoric, like this melancholy comparison of the poet's aging to a tree's shedding leaves:

>   now
> I that shed days, not by the season
> Alone but all the year round,

> Go without promise of fruits
> Decaying from my roots.

Clark's play The Boat is his first prose drama. Its prose implies that Clark has indeed turned to a more naturalistic literary mode. The plot is historical and better suited to prose than Clark's earlier drama. The subject is fratricide and justice under traditional law, and the time is seventy-five or more years in the past. Its principal characters are brothers who inherited a boat they share and quarrel to the death over, and a judge (Clark's ancestor) who was one of the members of the court that determined the fate of the murderer. The quarrel and the trial both are essentially materialistic, so Clark's choice of prose was natural and wise. The prose is often rich and rhythmic and, especially in ceremonial moments, incantatory. Throughout, the text is a good acting script, but it is rarely exciting reading. The plot line is thin for a full-length play.

The Boat confirms the darkness of Clark's view of life. Bitter anger, blood, pain, and retribution, interrupting joy and invalidating harmony, show that the heritage of The Masquerade is still strong. Not even the occasional laughter brightens, for the laughter is cynical. Clark's dramas evoke, but do not purge, pity and fear. They are appropriate, however, to Clark's time and place.

Clark's new prolific period has just begun, and it would be unwise to put too much emphasis on the first products as determinative of the future. His abiding concern for the traditions and life of the Delta, and particularly for the Kiagbodo tradition, will certainly be manifest in varying ways, and he will be a persistent critic of the society he lives in. And, no doubt, he will continue to find, as in "Herons at Funama," consolation in nature:

> If at the end of our days here,
> There is the chance of coming
> Again as all faiths attest,
> There is no talent I shall ask
> For more than to be able
> To walk, swim, and fly
> Like you, oh, herons
> At play on my waterfront!

Notes and References

Chapter One

1. Thurstan Shaw, Nigeria: Its archaeology and early history (London: Thames & Hudson, 1978), pp. 29, 37-51.
2. P. Amaury Talbot, The Peoples of Southern Nigeria (London: [Federal Government of Nigeria] Frank Cass, 1926, 1969), 1:154-55. The information about Mein is drawn from E. J. Alagoa, A History of the Niger Delta (Ibadan: Ibadan University Press, 1972), pp. 62-68, 74-75, 83-84.
3. The Ozidi Saga (Ibadan, 1977), p. xxii, hereafter referred to as Saga.
4. See photographs and discussion in Robin Horton, "A Note on Recent Finds of Brasswork in the Niger Delta," Odu 2 (1965):1, 76-91. Alagoa, History, (p. 65), says that the artifacts were probably not acquired as insignia of office, but the Benin origin of the mask objects is evident, whatever the occasion.
5. Alagoa, History, pp. 74-75. His source is J. W. Hubbard, The Sobo of the Niger Delta (Zaria, 1948), not available to this writer.
6. Alagoa, History, p. 72.
7. Philip E. Leis, Enculturation and Socialization in an Ijaw Village (New York: Holt, Rinehart & Winston, Inc., 1972).
8. Private communication. Other observations about Clark's early years are drawn from conversations and correspondence with Clark.
9. Achebe's chi concept is discussed by Awoonor in The Breast of the Earth (Garden City: Anchor/Doubleday, 1956), pp. 258-67, and by the present writer. See Wren, Achebe's World (Washington: Three Continents Press, 1980), pp. 42-45, 185 (includes bibliography).
10. Ozidi (London, 1966), p. 86; Three Plays (London, 1964), p. 127.
11. The Example of Shakespeare (London, 1970), p. 93.

12. Casualties (London, 1970).
13. A Reed in the Tide (London, 1965), p. 7. The poem is "Agbor Dancer."

Chapter Two

1. Poems (Ibadan: Mbari, 1961).
2. Song of a Goat (Ibadan, 1961). References to this play will be to the Three Plays text, as will references to The Masquerade and The Raft.
3. This characterization of Clark's technique is drawn from Michael J. C. Echeruo, who perhaps has expressed the matter better: "Clark's lyrics are a combination of the concrete circumstance, a personal problem and some lyrical gesture." Echeruo first remarked on the poems as "invariably of an 'occasional' nature." "Traditional and Borrowed Elements in Nigerian Poetry," Nigeria Magazine 89 (1966):150.
4. All poems discussed in this chapter have been reprinted in A Reed in the Tide and A Decade of Tongues (London, 1981) unless attention is called, in notes or in the text, to their not being so reprinted.
5. A personal communication from Clark sets the illness at 1956.
6. Four Modern West African Poets (New York: NOK Publishers, 1977), p.25. Egudu's comment is expressed in general terms for all of Clark's poetry, but Casualties is a different case, and Egudu does not discuss those poems.
7. Poems has "The souls of men are steeped . . . with wanton motions bedevilling . . . all night, thro' . . . for gadfly have at my back . . ." and "Yo" replaces "Io."
8. The text did not settle quickly, however. The Beacon text was reprinted with a few revisions in Poems, but the Poems text omitted Clark's marginal notes that usefully clarify the poem. A Reed in the Tide included only "Two Segments From Ivbie: IV, VI." The two segments are for the first (and only) time titled: "IV. A Town Asleep" and "VI. In the Cult of the Free." The segments lack marginal notes, but Clark provided endnotes that partially correspond to marginal notes but do not fit the segments published well. The A Decade of Tongues version, "Ivbie: A song of wrong," includes both the poem and marginal notes, without significant changes.
9. Black Orpheus 7 (June 1960):34-35, with seven

photographs inset, containing the commentary by Akanji. Not all Yoruba readers will agree with Akanji's identifications; it is likely his source was the artist.
10. M. J. C. Echeruo, private communication. He recalls that the head of department, Molly Mahood, offered the paper, but she does not agree.
11. Wilfred Cartey, Whispers from a Continent (New York, 1969), p. 346.
12. Robert G. Armstrong, "Song of a Goat," Ibadan 15 (March 1963):29-30.
13. Una Maclean, "Song of a Goat," Ibadan 14 (October 1962):28-29.
14. M. M. Mahood, "Drama in New-born States," Presence Africaine 60, no. 4 (1966; English Edition vol. 32):23-39.
15. Cyprian Ekwensi, Africa 10 (September 1965):2.
16. Scott Kennedy, In Search of African Theatre (New York: Chas. Scribner's Sons, 1973), p. 178. His comment seems to have been on the same Ghanaian performance called "only a melodrama" by Ossie Onuora Enekwe, "Africans and the Tragic Form," Greenfield Review 3, no. 4 (1974):35-36. The best production ever could have been M. J. C. Echeruo's at Nsukka in 1962. Unfortunately, Sunday Anozie's review (Daily Express, March 21, 1962, p. 3) is so favorable that one mistrusts his objectivity.
17. M. J. C. Echeruo, "Incidental Fiction in Nigeria," African Writer 1, no. 1 (August 1962):11.
18. Amber 2, no. 1 (August 1964):8-9; Black Orpheus 16 (October 1964):35-37.
19. The Sunday Express has not been available so only Daily Express articles are noted here. The articles commented on below were published October 30, November 4, and November 3, 1961.
20. America, Their America (London, 1964; Heinemann, 1968). The Heinemann text will be cited hereafter.

Chapter Three

1. Lest there be misunderstanding, these should be identified. Marguerite (Mrs. Herbert) McAneny, who died recently, was a good friend. The close relative is my late brother-in-law Hugh Boyd. The mentor (and dissertation reader) is the late Alan Downer (see

America, pp. 42-44, 87-90, 95-96). Of acquaintances mentioned in the book, the most significant is Dr. Robert van de Velde. Comments by van de Velde mentioned below and not drawn from Clark's book are recent personal communications.
   2. Report on "Parvin Fellows Program," submitted by Donald Easum, June 19, 1963. Seen at the Parvin Program office, Princeton University.
   3. William Connor, "Diribi's Incest: The Key to J. P. Clark's The Masquerade," World Literature Written in English 18, no. 2 (1979):278-86.
   4. Theo Vincent, "The Modern Inheritance: Studies in J. P. Clark's The Raft & Soyinka's The Road," Oduma 2, no. 1 (August 1974):39.
   5. "Interview with John Pepper Clark," in Bernth Lindfors et al., Palaver (Austin, Texas, 1972), p. 17.
   6. R. N. Egudu, "J. P. Clark's The Raft: The Tragedy of Economic Impotence," World Literature Written in English 15 (1976):297-304.
   7. Palaver interview, p. 17.

Chapter Four

   1. Unpublished communication, 1974 (on file, English Department, University of Lagos). Jituboh is a member of the Kabowei Clan in the Patani area, near both Clark's home and Orua, the place where the Ozidi story is said to have begun.
   2. J. B. Egberike, "J. P. Clark's Izon-English Translation of the Ozidi Saga," Kiabàrà 2 (1979):7. Egberike uses the more correct "Izon" for "Ijo"; a large part of the article is devoted to discussing Clark's orthography.
   3. Isidore Okpewho, The Epic in Africa (New York, 1979), passim. John William Johnson, "Yes Virginia, There is an Epic in Africa," Research in African Literatures 11 (1980):308-26.
   4. An example of a transcription which scarcely indicates the circumstances of performance is Daniel Biebuyck's The Mwindo Epic (Berkeley and Los Angeles: University of California Press, 1969). See, for example, p. 101, where a song is concluded incongruously "Muisa, you are helpless against Mwindo. / A bit of food, thanks, puts an end to a song." A footnote explains, "the narrator is invited to go eat and thanks

his host." The Mwindo epic and the Ozidi saga have much in common; Okpewho, Epic, has called attention to some of the correspondences, pp. 77, 110-11, 185-86, and passim.

5. Pere, according to E. J. Alagoa, "refers to the high priest of the national god of most Central and Western Delta ibe," or dialect groups. History of the Niger Delta, pp. 64, 15. Alagoa's discussion clearly implies that "high priest" is an inexact translation. The pere was a high political figure in a loosely shaped political formation. Clark hints at this in footnote 26, p. 206, when he mentions "the Pere, the Priest/King. . . ."

6. Okabou ascribes the same neonate taboo to Ogueren (p. 110), almost certainly an unintended repetition. Some footnotes to Night Three, it may be noted here, are scrambled. There are two 5s; the second repeats 3. Number 6 does not have a note; 7 should be 6, 8 should be 7, and I cannot find the "Song" to which note 8 refers.

7. Okpewho reminds readers that the visitation of the Smallpox King in the Saga is no divine intervention. He is, rather, the last of a long series of bumbling rivals, "slated for destruction just like all the others" (p. 5). Okpewho's study of the epic became available after this chapter was finished. Where his views are directly relevant to this study, they are parallel or confirmatory. Readers may find valuable comments about the Saga on many pages not indicated in Okpewho's index. Some of the more relevant references are pp. 102-3, 136, 157-59, 173-75, 193-94, 234, 250-51 (n. 42). Other useful relevant passages, particularly pp. 3-5, 200-201, are noted in his index.

Chapter Five

1. Kolawole Ogungbesan, "Nigerian Writers and Political Commitment," Ufahamu 5, no. 2 (1974):27.

2. A. Bodunrin, "Politics in Poetry," African Statesman 7, no. 1 (1972):17.

3. Quoted from Nigerian Outlook by Walter Schwartz, Nigeria (London: Pall Mall Press, 1968), p. 159.

4. John P. Mackintosh, Nigerian Government and Politics: Prelude to the Revolution (London: George Allen & Unwin, 1966), p. 554.

5. Quoted from the Daily Express by Schwartz, Nigeria, p. 175.

6. Daily Times, October 18, 1967, reports on testimony regarding bribery of a police superintendent for recruiting of thugs as police for use in controlling the 1965 election.

7. West Africa, October 16, 1965, p. 1151; see also the letter from the Chairman of the Electoral Commission E. E. Esua, Daily Express, November 20, 1965.

8. Chief Justice Olujide Somolu's tribunal on Western Region corruption revealed bribery with monotonous repetition. See Daily Times, October 12, 1967, for an example of one thousand five-pound notes being given over by hand. For the Archbishop's involvement, see Daily Times, September 15 and also September 7. The references are cryptic but meaningful.

9. Peter Thomas, "The Water Maid and the Dancer: Figures of the Nigerian Muse," Literature East and West 12, no. 1 (March 1968):85.

10. N. J. Miners, The Nigerian Army 1956-1966 (London: Methuen, 1971), p. 113.

11. Robin Luckham, The Nigerian Military: A Sociological Analysis of Authority & Revolt 1960-67 (Cambridge: Cambridge University Press, 1971), p. 39.

12. Martin J. Dent, "The Military and Politics: A Study of the Relations Between the Army and the Political Process in Nigeria," St. Anthony Papers 21, African Affairs 3, edited by Kenneth Kirkwood (Oxford: Oxford University Press, 1969), p. 128 and n. 34.

13. Christopher Okigbo, "Come Thunder," Black Orpheus 2, no. 1 (February 1968):7. "Hurrah for Thunder" follows, pp. 7-8.

14. Dan Izevbaye, "The Poetry and Drama of John Pepper Clark," in Bruce King, ed., Introduction to Nigerian Literature (Lagos, 1972), p. 165.

15. The account of Ifeajuna's actions is drawn from "Special Branch Report of the Events of 15 January 1966" in A. H. M. Kirk-Greene, Crisis and Conflict in Nigeria: A Documentary Sourcebook 1966-1969 (London: Oxford University Press, 1971), 1:115-24. Additional information from Luckham, Nigerian Military, pp. 20-24. Why Ifeajuna and Okafor drove to Enugu at all remains unclear.

16. Ezekiel Mphahlele, The African Image (London: Faber & Faber, 1974), pp. 260-62.

17. John de St. Jorre, The Brothers' War: Biafra and Nigeria (Boston: Houghton Mifflin Co., 1972), p. 32.
18. Luckham, Nigerian Military, pp. 249, 42. See Schwartz, Nigeria, pp. 131-34, for a vivid account of the May 25 riot and its result.
19. Miners, Nigerian Army, p. 91.
20. Dent, "Military and Politics," pp. 124-25.
21. Luckham, Nigerian Military, p. 104.
22. Dent, "Military and Politics," p. 131, fn. 40.
23. de St. Jorre, Brothers' War, p. 67.
24. Ibid., p. 86. He admits to accepting at one time the 30,000 figure, which became widely publicized after the civil war started, but he notes that Ojukwu's original claim was "more that 7,000 dead," a horrible but reasonably accurate figure.
25. Kirk-Greene, Crisis, pp. 63-65.
26. Ogungbesan, "Nigerian Writers," p. 27.
27. It would be appropriate here to correct an error in Tayo Olafioya's article "Public Poetry of West Africa: A Survey," Ufahamu 6, no. 1 (1975):92. Apparently writing from notes rather than a text, he has given this poem a new title and devised for it several new lines.
28. The Aburi dispute is far too complex for meaningful discussion here. See Kirk-Greene, Crisis, pp. 75-82, 312-49, 352-72. Schwartz, Nigeria, has a superficial summary, pp. 220-26. History may not be as kind to Gowon as Clark is in this poem and in "Night Song," but the poems were written without perspective on Gowon's nine-year rule. Clark's enthusiasm for Gowon must be understood partly in terms of Clark's position as a man of no major region--not North, East, or West. Nigerian Opinion, November 1966, commented: "Caught in the struggle for leadership between the 'big brothers,' the Mid-West cannot but argue the continuation of the federation as a condition of its own existence, in effect then, a form of enlightened self interest" (Kirk-Greene, Crisis, p. 312). Gowon was certainly the only hope the Mid-West seemed to have in 1967 for protection of its own vital interests. Clark reflects that circumstance.
29. R. N. Egudu, Modern African Poetry and the African Predicament (New York: Barnes & Noble; London: Macmillan, 1978), p. 108.

30. The weaverbird (<u>Ploceus cucullatus</u>) literally weaves, even using knots, a fat, bottle-shaped nest with its only entry at the bottom. The intricacy of the nest is astonishing.
31. de St. Jorre, <u>Brothers' War</u>, p. 171, describes the "plot" for which Ifeajuna, Agbam, and others were executed. The "<u>black-kite</u>" in the poem may be Ojukwu, who headed the <u>"flock"</u> Okigbo led into battle.
32. Ibid., facing p. 97; photo credit, pp. 8, 10. Also used on the book jacket, front.
33. The 1970 text, line 17, reads "some sixty years"; this is altered in 1981 to "many decades." The execution described in the poem is reported in the <u>Daily Telegraph</u> (London), June 27, 1968, and elsewhere.
34. Chinua Achebe, "Refugee Mother and Child," in <u>Beware Soul Brother and other poems</u> (Enugu: Nwankwo-Ifejika & Co., 1971), p. 8.
35. Personal communication.

Selected Bibliography

PRIMARY SOURCES

1. Autobiography
America, Their America. London: André Deutsch, 1964; Heinemann, 1968.

2. Essays
The Example of Shakespeare. London: Longman, 1970.

3. Plays
Song of a Goat. Ibadan: Mbari, 1961.
Three Plays. London: Oxford University Press, 1964.
Ozidi. London: Oxford University Press, 1966.

4. Poems
Poems. Ibadan: Mbari, 1961.
A Reed in the Tide. London: Longman, 1965.
Casualties. London: Longman, 1970.
A Decade of Tongues. London: Longman, 1981.

5. Translation
The Ozidi Saga. Ibadan: Ibadan and Oxford University Presses, 1977.

6. Film
Tides of the Delta (with Frank Speed).

7. Interviews
In African Writers Talking, edited by Dennis Duerden and Cosmo Pieterse. London: Heinemann, 1972.
In Palaver: Interviews with Five African Writers in Texas, edited by Bernth Lindfors, Ian Munro, Richard Priebe, and Reinhard Sander. Austin: University of Texas, 1972.

SECONDARY SOURCES

1. Bibliography
LINDFORS, BERNTH. Black African Literature in Eng-

lish: A Guide to Information Sources. Detroit: Gale Research Company, 1979. Indispensable.

2. Parts of Books

AKEYEA, E. OFORI. "Traditionalism in African Literature: J. P. Clark." In Perspectives on African Literature: Selections from the Proceedings of the Conference on African Literature Held at the University of Ife 1968, edited by Christopher Heywood. New York: Africana, in association with the University of Ife Press, 1971. Comment on Ozidi.

ASHAOLU, ALBERT OLU. "J. P. Clark: His Significance as a Dramatist." In Theatre in Africa, edited by Oyin Ogunba and Abiola Irele. Ibadan: Ibadan University Press, 1978. Thoughtful article, marred by misdating composition of The Raft.

CARTEY, WILFRED. Whispers from a Continent: The Literature of Contemporary Black Africa. New York: Random House, 1969. Includes useful discussion of Song of a Goat, pp. 340-50.

EGUDU, ROMANUS. Four Modern West African Poets. New York: Nok, 1977. Discusses Poems and A Reed in the Tide; does not include Casualties or drama. Major study.

EGUDU, R. N. Modern African Poetry and the African Predicament. London: Macmillan, 1978. Includes discussion of Clark's political poems in context of other poetry on similar themes.

IZEVBAYE, DAN. "The Poetry and Drama of John Pepper Clark." In Introduction to Nigerian Literature, edited by Bruce King. Lagos: University of Lagos and Evans Bros., 1971. Important basic study, inclusive to publication.

LAWRENCE, MARGARET. Long Drums and Cannons: Nigerian Dramatists and Novelists. New York: Frederick A. Praeger, 1969. Criticism of plays.

OKPEWHO, ISIDORE. The Epic in Africa: Toward a Poetics of the Oral Performance. New York: Columbia, 1979. Many insightful comments on The Ozidi Saga (index not reliable).

POVEY, JOHN. "Cannons of Criticism for Neo-African Literature." In Proceedings of a Conference on African Languages and Literatures held at Northwestern University April 28-30, 1966, edited by Jack Berry, Robert Plant Armstrong, and John Povey. Evanston: Northwestern University Press, 1966. Cites

Clark in defense of European criticism of African literature.
UDOEYOP, NYONG J. Three Nigerian Poets: A Critical Study of Soyinka, Clark and Okigbo. Ibadan: Ibadan University Press, 1973. Extended review of Clark's poetry through Casualties.

3. Journal Articles

ADEDEJI, J. A. "Some notes on Song of a Goat by J. P. Clark." Ibadan 28 (July 1970):99-101. Sympathetic review of non-Greek tragic background.

ADELUGBA, DAPO. "Trance and Theatre: The Nigerian Experience." Ufahamu 6, no. 2 (1976):47-61. Discusses Song of a Goat with reference to Ijaw mermaid rites.

ARMSTRONG, ROBERT G. "Song of a Goat." Ibadan 15 (March 1963):29-30. Review of original publication and performance.

ASHAOLU, ALBERT OLU. "The Tragic Vision of Life in The Raft." Obsidian 3, no. 3 (Winter 1977): 20-25. Sees human helplessness as central to Clark's early plays.

ASTRACHAN, ANTHONY. "Like Goats to the Slaughter: Three Plays by John Pepper Clark." Black Orpheus 16 (October 1964):21-24. Analysis of plays as classic tragedies.

BODUNRIN, A. "Politics in Poetry." African Statesman 7, no. 1 (1972):15-20. Sympathetic examination of Casualties in context of Nigerian crises.

BROWN, LLOYD W. "The American Image in African Literature." Conch 4, no. 1 (March 1972):55-70. On Clark's treatment of black middle class in America, Their America.

CONNOR, WILLIAM. "Diribi's Incest: The Key to J. P. Clark's The Masquerade." World Literature Written in English 18, no. 2 (1979):278-86. Original and significant study.

ECHERUO, M. J. C. "Traditional and Borrowed Elements in Nigerian Poetry." Nigeria Magazine 89 (June 1966):142-55. Brief but incisive comment on Clark's early poetry.

EGBERIKE, J. B. "J. P. Clark's Izon-English Translation of the Ozidi Saga." Kiabàrà 2 (1979):7-35. Critical philological study; cultural and linguistic context.

EGUDU, ROMANUS. "J. P. Clark as a Bastard Child: A

Study of 'Ivbie.'" Journal of the New African Literature and the Arts 13/14 (1973):21-26. Reexamines "bastard child" concept.
EGUDU, R. N. "J. P. Clark's The Raft: The Tragedy of Economic Impotence." World Literature Written in English 15, no. 2 (November 1956):297-304. Sociological implications of the play.
ESSLIN, MARTIN. "Two African Playwrights." Black Orpheus 19 (March 1966):33-39. Review article of Three Plays and Wole Soyinka's Five Plays, from consciously alien perspective.
FERGUSON, JOHN. "Nigerian Drama in English." Modern Drama 11, no. 1 (May 1968):10-26. Includes brief but valuable commentary on Three Plays.
IFIE, J. E. "Notes on Ezon Religion and Culture in the Ozidi Saga." Orita 12, no. 1 (1978):66-81. Occasionally overstated criticism of "mistranslation"; contains valuable cultural background information.
KENNARD, PETER. "Recent African Drama." Bulletin of the Association for African Literature in English 2 (1965):11-19. Perceptive commentary on Three Plays.
MCLOUGHLIN, T. O. "The Plays of John Pepper Clark." English Studies in Africa 18, no. 1 (March 1975): 31-40. Sets Ozidi in contrast to Three Plays; illuminating study.
NNOKA, BARBARA GRANT. "Authenticity in John Pepper Clark's Early Poems and Plays." Literature East & West 12, no. 1 (March 1968):56-67. Sets Clark in both European and African traditions; important study of A Reed in the Tide and Three Plays.
OBUKE, OKPURE O. "The Poetry of Wole Soyinka and J. P. Clark: A Comparative Analysis." World Literature Today 52, no. 2 (Spring 1978):216-23. Useful comment on well-known early poems.
OGUNGBESAN, KOLAWOLE. "Nigerian Writers and Political Commitment." Ufahamu 5, no. 2 (1974):20-50. Interesting for hostile commentary on Casualties.
O'MALLEY, (FATHER) PATRICK. "J. P. Clark and The Example of Shakespeare." Odi 3, no. 1 (1978):4-15. Examines Clark's critical theory.
POVEY, JOHN. "The Poetry of J. P. Clark: 'Two hands a man has.'" African Literature Today 1 (1968):36-47. Early, influential article.
SAINT-ANDRE-UTUDJIAN, ELAINE. "Clark's Use of Local Colour in The Masquerade." Commonwealth Essays and Studies 2 (1976):24-43. Discussion of localization techniques.

SOYINKA, WOLE. "A Maverick in America." Ibadan 22 (June 1966):59-61. Commentary on America, Their America (see Clark's response, Ibadan 23 [October 1966]:55).
THEROUX, PAUL. "Voices out of the Skull: a study of six African poets." Black Orpheus 20 (August 1966):41-58. Sensitive, brief discussion of a few poems.
THUMBOO, EDWIN. "An Ibadan Dawn: The Poetry of J. P. Clark." Books Abroad 44, no. 3 (Summer 1970):387-92. Includes an extended discussion of "Boeing Crossing."
UKA, KALU. "J. P. Clark's Ozidi: A Suggested Teaching Approach." Okike 13 (1979):84-92. For secondary schools.
VINCENT, THEO. "The Modern Inheritance: Studies in Clark's The Raft and Soyinka's The Road." Oduma 2, no. 1 (1974):38-41, 44-49. Existential problems in drama.

Index

Abubakar Tafawa Balewa, Sir, 133-36, 139-40
Achebe, Chinua, 9, 55, 77, 151-52, 155
Ado (Benin), 89-93
Afoluwa, 21, 88-91
Agbam, Sam, 128-29, 150, 170n31
Aguiyi-Ironsi, Major General J. T. U., 139, 142-45
Ahmadu Bello, Alhaji Sir, 135, 137-38, 140-41
Akintola, Chief Samuel A., 135, 139-40
Alagoa, E. J., 6
Amadi, Elechi, 46
Ambakederemo, 159
ancestors, 10, 72-73
aphorism. See rhetoric; riddles
Arena Stage (Washington, D.C.), 59
Armstrong, Robert G., 44
Atazi, 91
atom bomb, 82, 85. See also Cuban missile crisis
Auden, W. H., 20, 156
Awolowo, Chief Obafemi, 78, 83-84, 141
Awoonor, Kofi, 10
Azikiwe, Dr. Nnamdi, 83-85, 133
"Azudu Saga," 87

Bakederemo, Chief Clark Fuludu, 9, 21, 25

"bastard child," 32-34, 38, 59
Beacon, The, 23-24, 27, 52
Beier, Ulli, 39
Benin, 4-6, 9, 13, 89-91, 136, 139-40, 159
Biafra, 145
black Americans, 58, 62-65
Black Orpheus, 35, 39, 52
Blake, William, 27-28, 37
Bug, The, 37

Carter, Cyril, 22
Cartey, Wilfred, 44
Cary, Joyce, 115
chi. See teme
Clark, J. P., 1, 7, 17, 20-22, 23, 77, 83, 87, 127, 128-29, 136-37, 145, 154-55, 158

WORKS: DRAMA, 16, 20, 159, 161
Boat, The, 158-59, 161
Masquerade, The, 11-12, 14, 20, 51, 54, 69-76, 161
Ozidi, 9-11, 13, 14, 20, 21, 59, 87-127, 159
Raft, The, 14, 15, 54, 59, 69, 77-82
Song of a Goat, 10-12, 14, 20, 23, 40-

Index

51, 59-60, 69-70, 72-73

WORKS: FICTION, 51-52
"At the Waterfront," 52
"Stop in the Night, A," 52

WORKS: FILM (with Frank Speed)
Tides of the Delta, 92, 104-5. See also Ozidi (drama); The Ozidi Saga (translation)

WORKS: POETRY, 8, 16, 159-61
"Abiku," 35-36, 39-40
"Aburi and After," 148-49
"Addis Ababa," 156-57
"Agbor Dancer," 38
America, Their America, poems from, 68-70
"August Afternoon," 145
"Beast, The," 149, 153
"Benin Sacrifice," 151, 170n33
"Bombay," 157
"Burden in Boxes, The," 142-43
"Calcutta," 157
Casualties, 19, 22, 34, 82, 127, 128-57, 159
"Casualties, The," 151-52
"Cave Call," 83
"Cockerel in the Tale," 138-39, 144
"Conversation at Accra," 136, 140

"Cry of Birth, The," 25-26
"Death of a Weaverbird," 149-50, 170n30
Decade of Tongues, A, 83, 85, 146, 154, 157
"Dirge," 146-47
"Emergency Commission," 69, 83
"Epilogue to Casualties," 154-56
"Exodus," 145
"Flight Across Africa," 83
"Flood, The," 137, 147-48
"For granny, from hospital," 4, 24-25
"Friends," 150-51
"Fulani Cattle," 37-38
"God is a Cow, A," 157
"Here Nothing Works," 159
"His Excellency the Masquerader," 69, 83
"Horoscope," 38
"Ibadan Dawn," 38-39
"Imprisonment of Obatala, The," 20, 39-40
"Incident at the Police Station, Warri," 156
"Incidental Songs for Several Persons," 128, 156-57
"Ivbie," 18, 26-34, 164n8
"July Wake," 144-45
"Lagos-Ibadan Road before Shagamu, The," 156
"Lamp by my Window, A," 156
"Leader, The," 69, 83
"Leader of the Hunt, The," 136-37, 140, 142

"Letter from Kampala," 157
"Locust Hunt, The," 143
"My head fills out in fear," 23-25
"Nairobi National Park," 156-57
"Night Rain," 34-35
"Night Song," 130, 148
"On Faith," 27
"On the Theme of Child Wonder," 27
"Other Songs on Other States," 160
"Party Song," 151
"Photograph in the Observer, A," 151
"Plague, The," 160
"Players, The," 157
Poems, 23-40, 42, 83
"Progress," 160
"Rat in the Hole, The," 145
Reed in the Tide, A, 24, 30, 54-55, 68-69, 80, 82-86
"Reign of the Crocodile, The," 143, 153
"Retirement," 158
"Return Home," 142
"Ring round the Moon," 38
"Season of Omens," 131-36, 144, 153
"Skulls and Cups," 128-29, 131, 136, 148, 150
"Song," 130-31, 148, 150
"State of the Union," 160
State of the Union, 19, 158-61
"Streamside Exchange," 36-37

"Three Moods of Princeton," 85-86
"To my Academic Friends who sit tight on their Doctoral Theses and have no Chair for Poet or Inventor," 156
"Tree," 38
"Usurpation, The," 142
"Vulture's Choice," 131-32
"What the Squirrel Said," 143-44
"Who bade the Waves," 85

WORKS: PROSE NONFICTION
America, Their America, 53-70, 78, 83, 85, 159
"Aspects of Nigerian Drama," 115
Example of Shakespeare, The, 44, 59, 115-17
journalism (Express), 23, 52-54, 87
"Legacy of Caliban, The," 116

WORKS: TRANSLATIONS
Ozidi Saga, The, 5-8, 10-11, 13, 21, 22, 80, 87-127, 159
Clark's grandmother ("Granny"), 4, 7-8, 15, 21, 24-25
Connecticut (Wesleyan University), 22
Connor, William, 72
coups d'etat (1966), 84, 134-42, 144-45

Index

Cuban missile crisis, 60-61, 85

Defoe, Daniel, 115
Dent, Martin J., 136, 143
de St. Jorre, John, 151
Downer, Alan, 58, 165-66n1

East Central State, 155
Eastern Region, 133, 136, 139, 145-46
Echeruo, Michael J. C., 154-55, 164n3
Egberike, J. B., 89-90
Egudu, Romanus N., 25, 79, 150
Ekwensi, Cyprian, 45
Eliot, T. S., 27-28, 115
English language, 20, 44, 76, 93, 95-97, 115-16, 120
English rhetoric. See rhetoric
Erivini, 92, 105, 111-12, 114, 116-19
Express newspapers, 22, 52-53

Fajuyi, Lt. Colonel Adekunle, 144-45
family, 11, 72-73
folktales, 13-14, 114, 131
Forcados, 2, 3, 15, 73
Forcados River, 2, 4-6, 9, 21, 81
Funama, 158, 161

Ghana, 62, 140, 142, 148
Government College, Ughelli, 22
Gowon, Lt. Colonel Yakubu, 140, 144-45, 148-49, 151, 153, 169n28

Haile Selassie, 157
Hausa, 21, 146
Home News, The New Brunswick (N.J.), 57-58
Hopkins, Gerard Manley, 27, 38-39
Horn, The, 23-29, 38

Ibadan, 92, 135, 139, 144. See also University College, Ibadan; University of Ibadan; Mbari Club
Ifeajuna, Major Emmanuel A., 128-29, 136-37, 139-42, 147-48, 150, 152-55, 170n31
Igbo, 10, 21, 91, 113, 142-43, 146-47
Ijo, 1-16, 20-21, 35, 40-42, 44-47, 49-50, 54, 68, 73, 76, 87, 159
Ijo rhetoric. See rhetoric
impotence, 48
indirection, 43, 109, 121. See also rhetoric; riddles
Irele, Abiola, 26-27
Ironsi. See Aguiyi-Ironsi
Izevbaye, Dan, 137-38

Jituboh, V. C. O., 89, 166n1
Johnson, John William, 90

Kennedy, Scott, 45
Kiagbodo, 4-16, 20-22, 158, 161

Lagos, 22, 80, 133, 136, 138-39, 144, 159
Leis, Philip E., 7-13

McAneny, Marguerite, 58, 165n1
Maclean, Una, 44
Mahood, Molly M., 44-45, 165n10
Maimalari, Brigadier Zak, 139-40, 143
masseur, 11, 45-46
Mbari Club, Ibadan, 44-45
Mein, 4-9
mermaid. See water spirits
metaphor, 42-44. See also rhetoric; riddles
Mid-west Region, 136, 139, 145-46, 169n28
Mphahlele, Ezekiel, 140

negritude, 27-29, 33, 35
New York, 55-56, 60
Ngbile, 4-5, 9, 11
Ngbilebiri, 4-6, 8, 158
Ngugi, James, 156
Niger Company, 6, 81
Niger delta, 1-4, 73, 76-77, 96, 159
Niger River, 1-2, 14, 15, 73, 77-78, 155
Nigeria, 1, 17-21, 69, 77-78, 82, 128-56, 159
Nkrumah, Kwame, 142
Northern Region, 132-33, 135, 141, 145
Nwankwo, Nkem, 45
Nzeogwu, Major C. K., 138-39

Odutola, Ebun, 20-21
Oedipus Rex, 126
Ogidi, 155
Ogungbesan, Kolawole, 147
Ojukwu, Lt. Colonel O., 139-40, 144-45, 148, 155, 170n31
Okabu Ojobolo, 91-104, 111-12, 116-19, 122

Okigbo, Christopher, 128-29, 136-37, 140, 142, 145, 147-50, 152-53, 155

POEMS
"Come Thunder," 137, 168n13
"Hurrah for Thunder," 137
Okigbo, Dr. Pius, 143
Okotie-Eboh, Chief Festus, 109-10, 135-36, 139
Okpara, Dr. M. I., 140, 144
Okpewho, Isidore, 90, 167n7
Okrika (Ofonibengha), 21
Olafioya, Taya, 169n27
Onduku, Thomas, 21
Onitsha, 5, 53, 80, 85, 155-56
Oreame, 10. See also Clark, Ozidi; Ozidi Saga
Orua, 6-7, 9, 90, 96, 105
Osadebay, Chief Dennis, 144
Oyin, 10, 31-32, 124. See also Tamara
Ozobo, 91

parable. See rhetoric; riddles
Parvin Fellowship, 22, 54, 61. See also Clark, America, Their America
PEC Repertory Theatre, 22
pere, 9, 11, 96, 167n5
pidgin English, 113, 120
Poro (Clark's mother), 21
Prime Minister (Nigeria). See Abubakar Tafawa Balewa

Index

Princeton, 63-64
Princeton University, 56, 78. See also Clark, America, Their America

Readers' Union, 22
rhetoric, 116-26
riddles, 14, 42-44, 121. See also rhetoric

sacrifice, 48
Sardauna of Sokoto. See Ahmadu Bello
se. See teme
Shakespeare, William, 13, 42, 51, 74, 82, 108, 114-16, 118, 121-23, 125
songs, 14-15
Songs from "The Ozidi Saga" (recording), 87-88, 126
Soyinka, Wole, 35, 45
Speed, Frank, 87. See also Clark, Tides of the Delta
story form, 12-13
Student Union (University College, Ibadan), 19, 136, 154-55
Synge, John Millington, 20, 41

Tamara, 9-10, 112, 124-25
Tarakiri, 6-7
teme, 10

tortoise, trickster, 13, 113-14, 119-20
tragedy, 40-41, 49-51, 73

Ugo, Francis R., 7-16
University College, Ibadan, 18, 22, 57, 136, 154
University of Ibadan, 20, 22, 87, 127, 155
University of Lagos, 17, 22, 127, 158
University of Nigeria, Nsukka, 155
Urhobo, 4, 7-8, 15-16, 21, 28

van de Velde, Robert, 57-59, 61, 63, 165-66n1

Wali, Obiajunwa, 27, 128-29
Washington Post, the, 58, 61, 78
water spirits, 10, 46, 73, 103-4, 113, 118
Wenger, Suzanne, 39
Western Region, 78, 83, 132-34, 140, 145-46
wrestling, 111

Yabuku, Madame, 91-92, 94
Yeats, William Butler, 20, 41-43, 73
Yoruba, 19-21, 30, 35, 40, 146, 151